AROCHUKWU: A PATRIARCH'S REFLECTIONS

By George M. Onwuchekwa Esq.

(Ugwu-Aro)

Compiled 2019

DARUDAN PUBLISHING

First Published April 2020

By Darudan Publishing

Milton Keynes, Buckinghamshire, U.K

Copyright © 2020 Joseph Amaeze

The right of Joseph Amaeze to be identified as owner of this work has been asserted by him in accordance with sections 77 and 78 of the Copyright, Designs and Patents Act 1988.

All rights reserved. No part of this book may be reprinted or reproduced or utilised in any form or by any electronic, mechanical, or other means, now known or hereafter invented, including photocopying and recording, or in any information storage or retrieval system, without permission in writing from the publishers.

Trademark notice: Product or corporate names may be trademarks or registered trademarks, and are used only for identification and explanation without intent to infringe.

ISBN: 978-0-9935860-3-3

Edited by Joseph and Isoken Amaeze

Printed in Great Britain by Lightning Source UK Ltd

Cover design: Joseph Amaeze & ViknCharlie

CONTENTS

1. AROCHUKWU MARRIAGE CUSTOM
2. AROCHUKWU: LAND OF MY BIRTH
3. AROCHUKWU: GOLDEN YEARS
4. OKENNACHI KINDRED
5. AROCHUKWU BURIAL CUSTOM
6. GEORGE MOSES ONWUCHEKWA ODYSSEY

FOREWORD

My father was a great story teller, historian, poet with a great sense of humour. The sound of his laughter still resonates in my heart and mind. It was the sort of full belly laugh that engulfed his entire being and permeated his surroundings in such a way that those in its vicinity instinctively joined in. As Children, he often told my brother and I stories about the tortoise "Nnanna Mbe" as we sat at his feet captivated. Childhood moral lessons were illustrated by the many – often invented antics that this crafty tortoise got up to.

Dad truly was eloquent and also skilled in the art of non-verbal communication; especially by way of his facial expressions. He loved words and exhaustively shared every word God gave him both orally and through his writings. His wit was second to none and he could express the most complex issues in their most banal form without ceasing to captivate his audience. These were some of the qualities that made him such a marvellous educator and mentor in the home, community and professionally.

His passion for helping others coupled with an eagerness to share his insights and knowledge with them is a key driving force behind the writings compiled in this book. In 1993 gingered by my brother and having successfully gone through this process as a parent of the bride just two years prior - dad wrote the book Arochukwu Marriage Custom. It is the first and most referenced of all the works he humbly termed "guides". I highly recommend it to anyone seeking to learn about or contemplating a traditional marriage to an Arochukwu daughter.

My dad never passed up an opportunity to recount his memories of the beloved land of his birth Arochukwu. In the section titled Land of my birth originally written in 1994, he takes the reader on an epic journey to Arochukwu - as seen through his eyes in the first 16 years of life. It is here he introduces the legendary and unparalleled Aroman - of whom I would consider him to be among the cream of the crop.

He gave of himself to the service of others in a selfless manner that is worthy of emulation.

Arochukwu and its affairs held a central focus for him and a place in his heart. He was very fond of Arochukwu and had its culture and traditions deeply ingrained in him.

It was the land of his birth and always "Home" regardless of his physical residence. So he welcomes you as you embark on a journey to this land with his memoirs as your most able guide.

To God Almighty be all Glory and Adoration for the gift of Barrister George Moses Onwuchekwa Number One Dad.

Grace-Julia Okoroji (Nee Onwuchekwa}

AROCHUKWU MARRIAGE CUSTOM

By Barrister George M. Onwuchekwa Esq.

(Iyi-Ukwu Obinkita)

Written: 1993

PREFACE

I have been motivated to write and publish in pamphlet or booklet form, my personal understanding of the Arochukwu Marriage Custom, because of the inquiries which I very often receive from Arochukwu young men and women. As the Legal Adviser of Nzuko Arochukwu Lagos Branch, I explain to them what has to be done and the procedure to be taken for a formal Customary Marriage in Arochukwu. I will explain to them that although I am a lawyer, that I am not an authority on Arochukwu Custom. However, I inform them that whatever I say to them should only be taken as a guide and would be subject to whatever their elders tell them at Arochukwu, as there are family variations and even village variations or adaptations due to inroad made on Arochukwu Custom by contact with other towns and tribes where the Aros live which make such variation inevitable.

I have searched in vain for books or literature on Arochukwu Custom written by Arochukwu people. I have also discovered that the Aros are not eager to write about themselves. Hence, there are few books on Arochukwu history, culture, tradition and general behavioural pattern. Whatever has been written about Arochukwu has been written by the old Colonial Masters, outsiders and Aros in diaspora. Even the one time attempt by joint effort to produce a book on Arochukwu history which would have been the 'Magnus Opus' of Arochukwu history was aborted. So I was persuaded by son, Barrister Joseph Amaeze Onwuchekwa to put my personal knowledge and experiences which spans over 5 decades into writing since oral tradition alone is no longer stable and reliable as many knowledgeable elders are day by day joining their ancestors.

So I boldly decided to write his pamphlet in the hope that it would enkindle both responsible criticisms, and motivation for other town folks versed in the knowledge of Arochukwu Custom and culture to write distinguished books on

Arochukwu not only on its Marriage Customs but on every other aspect of Aroman. The social heritage of our distinguished and accomplished forefathers should not be allowed to die in obscurity. Therefore to all who may read this pamphlet, this is a guide.

GEORGE M. ONWUCHEKWA ESQ
Festac Town, Lagos
1993

TABLE OF CONTENTS

CHAPTER ONE

AROCHUKWU MARRIAGE CUSTOM

1. Preliminary
2. Ikutu-aka nuzo (knocking on the doors of the girl's parents)
3. Mmai Ububo (wine meant for discussion between the proposed in-laws)
4. Mmai-Ajuju (The Public Consent of the girl)
5. The Delegation
6. Aju-Mmai
7. Ikoyi-akpa
8. The Ceremony of Mmai Ajuju
9. Ikwa-Ani
10. In Search of the Husband
11. Mmai – Ihu Onu Aku
12. Mmai – Ukwu (Main Wine)
13. Taking the Bride away
14. Traditional gifts by Son-in-Law

CHAPTER TWO

Settlement of Marriage Disputes

(a) Matrimonial Conciliation and Appeasement
(b) Ruling (Decision)
(c) Divorce (Achokwam)
(d) The Customary Court

CHAPTER THREE

Uziship in Arochukwu

CHAPTER ONE

AROCHUKWU MARRIAGE CUSTOM

The historic and ancient town of Arochukwu – the land of the Long-juju or Ibinukpabi is rich in tradition, culture and customs which in most cases have not been dented or polluted by the so-called modern civilization. One area or aspect of Arochukwu social life which has stood the test of time is the institution of traditional or customary marriage.

In Arochukwu, like most Igbo towns and indeed most towns of Nigeria, marriage is a family affair, a village affair and a town affair as opposed to an individual affair. In most Western countries, marriages could be contracted by the couple themselves with one or two close friends from both sides as witnesses. Such marriages could be solemnized in the church or Marriage Registry once the couple are of full age which is now generally eighteen years of age to the exclusion of parental consent, knowledge or even invitation to the ceremony.

Such marriages, which in African terms may be likened to concubinage, are rarely sustained since they have little or no root and the rate of divorce in some countries is as high as fifty percent. You owe no obligation to any one, there is no call-to-order by any one and there is no relation to whom the young married couple may turn to for advice or encouragement save for the so-call Marriage Guidance Counsellors some of whom have no better marital life than their pupils. Such superficial advice based on the economy, temperament and compatibility alone only serve as palliative but fails to sustain or prop the marital relationship. Arochukwu traditional mode of marriage, on the other hand, has been tailored to cement the bond of marriage and family life unlike under some laws, where divorce is effective immediately on the pronouncement by a party thereto, a few times of 'The Magic Word'.

In this discussion, I would attempt to guide the reader through the main procedure or steps for effective and successful Arochukwu Traditional Marriage. I must however warn at this stage that there may be local, village or family variations which may be due to contact with other towns or tribes. Such variations (if any) do not derogate from the authenticity of the procedure (steps) and customary rites associated with the institution of Arochukwu Traditional Marriage but are inevitable aberrations of the social order, due to contact with outsiders – it must be remembered that Arochukwu have settlements in various parts of the Igbo land and great travellers. This may be regarded as acquired culture.

In addition, many Arochukwu people today, regard customary marriage as a first step towards marriage in the Church or Marriage Registry because of the protection it affords the wife and children. Customary or Traditional Marriage to these classes of people now becomes a link (although an important link) in the road to full solemnization of marriage instead of what it used to be, what it is and what it will forever remain a full-fledged marriage in itself, recognised by Nigerian Law. Church or Marriage Registry, therefore, is an additional cement in the bond of marriage because of the protection which it gives to the wife and children as to the inheritance of property and other related matters.

I will now discuss step by step the procedural requirements of effective customary marriages in Arochukwu.

Preliminary:

Young man finds a girl and introduces her to his parents and the girl does the same thing with her parents. The parents of each side through friends or relations will conduct subtle investigation about the other side. I said 'the other side', because not only the young man or woman are investigated, but their parents and near relations. Matters for which subtle questions may be asked or enquiries conducted are: whether either of the young man's parents is a thief or tabooed by Arochukwu Custom, whether either mother has been known to have committed adultery whilst in marriage; whether the relationship of either parents with brothers and sisters, village or town is cordial – as you do not want your son or daughter to inherit quarrel or enmity which may spread to you; whether the girl herself has been known to be a flirt; whether the history of childbirth is good etc. These are in addition to the economic circumstance and social standing of either party depending on their level of existence. These factors often overlooked nowadays by young men and women are perhaps some of the factors if discovered later may lead to breakdown of marriage.

A young man, who has seen a girl he wants to marry, usually would not just tell his father, 'I have seen a girl to marry'. He says so kneeling down besides his father or whosoever he looks up to as a father with full bottle of Schnapps and a container of ground tobacco to show his seriousness. He will give some lengths of leaves of unground tobacco, and a small container of ground tobacco with five shillings (50 Kobo) to his mother or the person he considers as his mother. Sometimes, he may give a fathom of cloth to his mother to show that he has come of age. These gifts (not the cloth) will be shared by his parents with other relations when they are contacted to begin the process of subtle investigation of the girl's background.

Sometimes, it is not the young man who is eager to find a wife. Many young men are not eager to marry as they prefer to be 'Okokporo' (bachelor). Some prosperous parents who want to set-up their son will take it upon themselves, without consulting their son, to conduct a subtle investigation of his friends' stables and other families, as to whether there is a girl who is marriageable but unmarried. He would ask some or all the questions stated above. Such girl, when found, would be imposed on the young man as wife and in those days, he had little or no say in the matter. Arochukwu parents of old would prefer marriages within their own caste (Ikwuu) which was matrilineal. Survivors of this caste system are still found in Arochukwu in the form of Ikwuu Azuma Eze; Ikwuu Nmaku; Ikwuu Eni, etc. where there is no suitable girl within the caste, the father will look among his friends' stables (homes). Having located a 'good girl' and informally discovering that the young man's parents' overtures will not be rebuffed, the parties proceed to step one of the marriage procedure.

STEP ONE:

'Ikwutu-aka nuzo' (knocking on the doors of the girl's parents)

This is the beginning of the official or formal part towards the ceremony of marriage. The parents of the girl are informed of the visit in advance. Usually, the Aros do not conduct serious family matters such as marriages, burials, etc. on Nkwo market day. A date for the visit would be Eke, Orie or Afor market days. This is the first face to face meeting between the proposed in-laws when the boy's father will officially ask if the girl is available for marriage and if she is, he discloses to her parents his intention to take her into his stable (marry her).

Usually, the topic will start by the boy's father saying to the girl's parents that he had located a girl (usually called by a pseudonym 'nwa-ewu' (well-nourished goat) in his stable. The boy's father will then present a bottle of Schnapps called 'Mmai-Ihe avuru n'ulo', which means the wine to indicate what I have found in your house. This activity takes place in consonance with Arochukwu traditions, after the presentation and breaking of kolanut presented by the father of the girl to welcome his visitors. There is no fanfare or publicity in this aspect of discussion, as there is not as yet any commitment by either side, so that, if the girl had in fact been betrothed to another man, the new suitor will not feel rejected.

To guard against publicity, only few close relatives on both sides are present (the matter is still within the house). Various questions – formal questions may now be asked by both sides to hear from the horse's mouth as it were, what they had been told confidentially by well-wishers.

Where a father has several daughters and is not very sure which of them is wanted, he will call them before him one after the other under the guise of sending them messages, e.g. 'please bring drinking water', 'go and buy snuff (ground tobacco) for me, etc. after the particular girl had come and gone out for her errand, the boy's father will indicate that she is the chosen one. Then the girl's parents will say, 'I would like to have time to ask my daughter and my relatives and if it is okay on our side, we will send back our reply. An Aroman never accepts immediately as this may portray him as being too eager to give his daughter away or too gluttonous. Arochukwu man does not sell his daughter in the guise of marriage. After some days, the girl's father will send down message to his proposed in-laws that the coast is now clear for the Mmai-Ububo, i.e. the next step in the procedure.

STEP TWO:

MMAI UBUBO (Wine meant for discussion between the proposed in-laws)

On the particular day mutually agreed between the proposed in-laws, the boy's parents and few close relations will go to the home of the proposed in-laws with drinks and other established gifts for the purpose of holding discussion, as to what both parties expect should be the future conduct of affairs between them in connection with proposed marriage – whether the girl will be in the fattening room (Mgbede) in due course; whether there would be future church marriage between their children, their future relationship with each other and in fact all aspects of the proposed marriage. All issues are discussed and bargained for. The conclusion of this stage or step will determine whether or not other marriage steps are to be taken. The whole exercise could if not properly handled, abort at this stage. The traditional presents given to the girl's parents are:

FATHER:
1 bottle of Scotch whisky
1 leg (hind leg) of dried meat (Utaku ani Okpo) and
2 gallons or kegs of palm wine (Itotuu mmai ukwu)

MOTHER:

1 bottle of Schnapps (Aromantick)
1 arm (front leg) of dried meat (Aka ani Okpo) and
1 gallon (keg) of palm wine (also called itotuu mmai nta)

The gifts meant for the Mmai-Ubobo are not refundable in the event that the proposed marriage negotiation is aborted.

After successful conclusion of the tête-à-tête, in the olden days, it used to be common practice to decide when the young virgin may be taken away by the boy's mother for living and working alongside her for an agreed period of time for the purpose of studying her manners, adaptability to hard work, cleanliness, susceptibility to flirting with other young men around the family etc. The living-in period (nkuru na nkulata) also affords the girl first-hand knowledge of the kind of family she is coming to and the temperament of the would be mother-in-law.

A hot drink is given before the girl may be taken away and if all goes well, on her return to her parents, another hot drink (Schnapps) is given to her parents and loads of gifts are given to her and her mother. The assortment and quality of same will indicate whether or not the proposed husband's family are happy with her. The marriage can be aborted at this stage without consequences on either side. This is the reason why the girl would be strongly advised by her mother not to sleep with the proposed husband. The boy's mother also guards the young girl jealously from her son – the proposed husband and from other men. The girl's mother is greatly distressed should her daughter come back pregnant – even if the marriage in the end is solemnized. This leads to great quarrel between the proposed in-laws but in the end, is settled in the Aroman's fashion. Today, because of schooling (education) and the need for every girl to improve herself before marriage, this aspect of taking the girl away for study rarely take place and has in fact become obsolescent – since almost all Arochukwu girls now go to school, at least up to the First School Leaving Certificate. Many girls go beyond the First School Leaving Certificate although, some may never complete due to shortage of funds or academic and social rascality.

STEP THREE:

MMAI-AJUJU: (The public consent of the girl)

Mmai-Ajuju as the name implies means the public questioning of the would-be-bride by her father and mother in turn in the presence of all relations on both sides, friends, well-wishers and others as to whether or not she actually wants to marry a particular man since the parents would not want to receive any presents from the in-laws attendant to the marriage, only to vomit or disgorge same because of the girl's behaviour. I will come back to this aspect later.

Mmai-Ajuju is one of the most significant phases (steps) of Arochukwu marriage custom. It is the first public appearance of both sides in the presence of all friends and well-wishers to transact the ceremony of marriage negotiation. Whereas, knocking on the door (Mmai ihe avuru n'ulo) and (Mmai Ububo) negotiation, (conversation or discussion) may be held outside Arochukwu Town where the parents of the girl reside e.g. Lagos, Aba, Port Harcourt, Kano etc. the Mmai-Ajuju should be performed at Arochukwu town. It is a taboo for this and the following stages or steps of customary marriage to be held outside Arochukwu town for an Arochukwu daughter. If for any reason (e.g. poor health) the actual father, if alive cannot travel to Arochukwu, it is always the Aro Custom for a close elder male relation to be mandated by him to act as putative father in this stage and subsequent stages of the marriage ceremony so however, that all the gifts will be passed on to the real father.

What is said here only applies to Aro-uno (or Aro-ulo) and Aros in diaspora who completely identify themselves with Arochukwu town and does not apply to Aro settlements which are deemed for this purpose to represent Arochukwu town for marriage ceremonies. But, no matter from where the suitor of an Arochukwu girl hails (Yoruba, other Igbos, Efik, Hausa, Edo etc.), the Mmai-Ajuju should be held at Arochukwu, where the girl is from Arochukwu town as opposed to merely being an 'Aro'. Various articles mainly consumables are required to be produced by the son-in-law and his delegation but before I list out the requirements, it is necessary to describe in brief the delegation which accompany the bridegroom to add pump colour and pageantry to the whole celebration.

THE DELEGATION:

The bridegroom's family will select from amongst their number and close relation, twelve (4 women and 8 men) to be the official delegation to their in-laws' place. The bridegroom also comes along with the official delegation smartly dressed in Arochukwu attire of Indian-madras loin cloth (George material of Omu-Aro – special designed Aro cloth) with a well-tailored jumper on top (preferably Isi-inyinya). The male delegation is also attired in similar fashion. It is an insult to the girl's family for the bridegroom and his official delegation to wear trousers, babariga etc. for this occasion or to be slovenly dressed. The women wear loin cloths of Indian-madras (George cloth) preferably Omu-aro, where this is available. It must be pointed out that although traditionally the official delegation are twelve, yet in practice this could be any number depending on the social standing of the parties and their ability to entertain and moreso, whether or not it is intended to perform the ceremonies of 'Mmai-Ajuju' and 'Mmai-Ukwu' (main wine) the same day in which event, the official delegation may be fourteen. In addition to the official delegation, other village men and women who are well-wishers of the bridegroom also follow in the procession to the bride's family as a mark of solidarity and to signify to all-comers and the public at large, the importance of what is being done.

Today, it is usual to combine on the same day, the ceremonies of Mmai-Ajuju and Mmai-Ukwu (the main wine) one ceremony, following the other but each maintaining its position as a separate step. However, where the bridegroom cannot afford to meet the obligations of both steps on the same day, a new date would be agreed between the in-laws which may be several months or even years in between.

Where it is intended to combine the two stages on the same day, the various articles required for the main wine (Mmai-Ukwu) will also be brought along by the same delegation in procession although things like palm wine and other drinks would have been discreetly stored by the groom in the in-law's house or that of a near relation. I will come back to the requirements of Mmai-Ukwu (main wine) but in the meantime, I am writing on the assumption that both Mmai-Ajuju and Mmai-Ukwu (main wine) ceremonies are to be performed on the same day by the same delegation. If this is the case, some of the requirements for the 'Mmai-Ukwu' will be carried or seen to be carried by the delegation in procession.

AJU-MMAI (Woven rings or pads dried plantain leaves)

Six able-bodied and well clad young men each carrying an Aju-mmai, lead the delegation followed in close proximity by six women properly attired each carrying a small wooden trough or metal tray each containing a symbolic amount of the bride price since this may not be known at this stage although everybody has a well-informed idea of the amount and these are covered with white serviette-like material (atumakasa). The women are then followed by the official delegation of men, each carrying a long walking stick of the height of about five feet six inches, in a way, depicting the traveller of old who had come from a long and tedious journey in search of precious commodity in this instance the bride. Most other men not in the official delegation carry the normal walking stick which is a part of Aro man's dressing (of loin cloth, jumper, hat and walking stick). The women in the procession would from time to time during their journey let out joyous cry of 'Ayoo' as a mark of happiness, solidarity and to herald their presence through all the villages or compounds they pass.

IKOYI-AKPA (Hanging up travel bags and kits)

When the procession arrives the bridegroom's compound, they do not go straight to the venue for the Mmai-Ajuju or Mmai-Ukwu, but will be received by a small delegation of the bridegroom's family and taken to the house of the person previously arranged for briefing, hanging up their travel bags or kits, refreshing up and short rest – after all, they have come from a wearisome journey. The owner of the house who may be a member of the family of the bride would be appointed their chief negotiator and spokesman. He being the 'son-of-the-soil' knows his people, their custom and idiosyncrasy. After a brief entertainment of kola-nut, cold water, soft drinks and beer, the delegation proceeds also in single files to the house of their in-laws or the venue for the ceremonies. It is necessary that they are officially received by their in-laws and ushered in. However, before the delegation steps into the in-law's house, they are expected to light the 'Ulo-Nta' (family house) by lighting a lamp since marriages in traditional Arochukwu setting (now nowadays) were conducted in the evening. This is called 'Imui Oku Ogbiti'. In actual fact it is only a symbolism as no lamp is lit but a payment of between one Naira to ten Naira is made to the in-laws.

The Aju-mmai (dried plantain leaf-pads or rings) are not brought or dropped as is required by custom at this stage but left in the house of the person where the delegation, hung-up their travel bags – this is the case where the ceremony of Mmai-Ajuju has not taken place. Aju-Mmai is for the Mmai-Ukwu (main wine) ceremony. Where however, the Mmai-Ajuju had already taken place on an earlier occasion, as soon as the delegates arrive at their in-laws' house, four (Aju-mmai) will be dropped with force to produce a deep loud noise in the front (forecourt) of the father-in-law's house (nearest the walls of the house), whether or not the ceremony of Mmai-Ukwu (main wine) is to take place outside, in the forecourt of the house, or compound square. The two remaining Aju-mmai are dropped in front of the mother-in-law's part of the house.

In the olden days, wives had their respective 'Usokwuu' exclusive part of the house which served for residence with kitchen attached – usually an outhouse. In modern times there may not be such separation between the husband and wife and so her two 'Aju-Mmai' will be dropped behind the family house nearest the kitchen which now serves as her 'Usokwuu'. I will refer to Aju-Mmai again during the 'Mmai-Ukwuu' (main wine) ceremony – its proper place.

THE CEREMONY OF MMAI-AJUJU:

As it has been said earlier, the ceremony of 'Mmai-Ajuju' is the first public ceremony in the course of Arochukwu traditional or customary marriage. When the delegation and guests are seated, there would be presentation of kola-nuts, bitter-kola, garden eggs (ikete or anara) with Okwu-ose (a sort of spiced peanut butter) and 'ose-oji' (alligator pepper), a bottle of Schnapps hot drink, a keg of palm wine and assorted soft drinks, stout, malt drink and beer, by the father-in-law to the delegation to welcome them in the Arochukwu tradition. What is offered will depend on the ability of the girl's family.

The type of kola-nuts used are the Igbo kola-nuts (Oji-Igbo) as opposed to 'gworo' (Oji-Awusa). There will be four or eight 'Oji-Igbo' in addition to the garden eggs. But, before the kola-nuts are shared and libation poured by the girl's father, grandfather or elder relation, there would be formal introduction of the parties, starting with the official delegation of the bridegroom and then the girl's family. The women are seated in front of the mother-in-law's 'Usokwuu' (part of the back building) where they will be similarly presented with their own kola-nuts and other drinks.

After exchanges of pleasantries, the official ceremony of 'Mmai-Ajuju' (public consent by the girl) would begin. Each side has a spokesman. Usually the bride's relation whose house was used as a staging-post (Ikoyi-akpa) will act as the spokesman of the bridegroom and another male member of the bride's family (and not the father) is appointed the spokesman of the bride's family. Because the negotiation and bargaining are in effect conducted by and between relatives (one of them on behalf of the outsiders), there is always great humour and cordiality, although the bargain is usually tough. The spokesman of the bridegroom is transformed notionally into a native of the bridegroom's village or town and is addressed throughout the ceremony as such, amidst great laughter and shared jokes. Then the spokesman of the bride's family will, standing up, formally welcome his counterpart who also is standing and ask him what he had come for (although already known by all). He will answer by saying that he has come to perform the 'Mmai-Ajuju' and that also, if his in-laws permit, that he intends and is ready and willing to complete all the ceremonies of the institution of marriage the same day, one following the other. Then, the spokesman of the bride's family will thank him for his ability to perform but would jokingly inform him that whether or not he would be allowed to proceed to other stages of marriage ceremony would depend on the successful outcome and his ability to satisfy his side in the 'Mmai-Ajuju ceremony.

The bride's father's spokesman now turns to the bride's father and publicly asks him one after the other whether his in-laws have knocked on his door (Ikutu-aka nuzo) and whether they have satisfied him in connection with 'Mmai-Ububo' (wine meant for the discussion between the proposed in-laws). After he has answered in the affirmative, his spokesman will then ask the spokesman of the bridegroom to show his hand, i.e., to produce all the requirements for the 'Mmai-Ajuju' ceremony. These are:

For the Bride's father:
i. One bottle of Scotch-whisky (three-in-one)
ii. One leg (hind leg) of dried meat (Utaku Ani Okpo)
iii. Two gallons or large kegs of palm-wine (Itotu-mmai)

For the Bride's Mother:

i. One bottle of Schnapps (Aromantick)
ii. One arm (front leg) of dried meat (Aka Ani Okpo)
iii. One gallon (keg or small Itotu) of palm wine.

The above items with the exception of the palm wine are put in different trough or metal trays (okwa) meant for her father and mother respectively but on the tables or stools. The parents of the bride would not touch these things nor present them to their family unless their daughter publicly confirms that it is her wish to marry. At this stage, the father sends for his daughter but since a child is made by man and woman, the women, to show their power and to buttress their position as joint partners in birth and marriage, would send for the bridegroom's spokesman through the family spokesman (never direct) they then inform him, that unfortunately the girl is away in a different land or even overseas in Europe and that they require air fare and money for other modes of local transportation for the purpose of going to bring her back.

Women never give in and their negotiation and bargaining is so tough but, in the end, a sum of money is agreed upon between them and handed over before the women troop out to bring the bride who has been properly dressed up for the occasion as is befitting in Arochukwu tradition, the bride being led by young maiden dancers, followed by her mother, other female relations and women relations of her proposed husband. When she approaches the venue, all well-wishers will shower her with praises and monetary gifts which are picked from the ground by her hand-maiden (bridesmaid) who may be a good friend or a younger female relation. There is great joy and jubilation showering of praises for her and her mother regularly punctuated with the joy cry of 'Ayoo'. She is expected to dance in a maiden-like manner carrying herself with dignified composure and smiles which then further generates presentation of money by the friends of both families (men and women) on her forehead.

When the bride has been led into the arena, she is embraced and welcomed by her father and is given a seat beside her father in a pre-decorated chair set aside for that purpose. The chair is usually decorated with Indian-madras cloth (George cloth) including the floor on which she rests her legs. Her father will praise her and also with the members of his family, shower her with monetary gifts. After the bride has adjusted to her chair, her family spokesman will hand over to her, the trough or tray containing the items meant for her father which was brought by her proposed husband and would ask her to present same to her father. She then gets up to receive same and, kneeling in front of her father as a sign of respect and good family upbringing, she then hands over the tray to her father. The father first will ask her who brought the gifts and she would reply. She would reply that the gifts had been brought by a man who intends to marry her. Then her father will publicly ask her whether she knows the purpose of the gifts. If her reply is yes, her father will finally ask her whether it is her wish to be so married, i.e. whether she gives her consent as he does not want to accept the gifts only to disgorge same (since an Aroman does not sell his daughter or give away in marriage an unwilling daughter). If her answer is in the affirmative, her father will thank her and accept the items which he passes back to the spokesman to be shared. She will also carry her mother's tray and in the presence of the women folk is subjected to the same questions by her mother.

Ikwa-Ani:

It is significant that when the trays containing the various items are placed on the respective tables, but before the bride is invited into the arena, the bride's family (men on their part and women on their part) will inspect the dry meat as to its size, degree of dryness and suitability. The palm-wine is also tested. Usually, the meat is ruled to be under size and not suitable and the palm-wine sour. This calls for monetary augmentation of the meat and for the improvement in the taste of the palm-wine to the bride's family. Women are more difficult in their bargaining for the amount of money required for the augmentation of the dried meat and for the improvement in the taste of the palm-wine. In yesteryears, only a token sum of money was required of the son-in-law but today, it could be high — sometimes this could call for the intervention of the men folks of the bride's family to remind the women that their daughter is not being sold and moreover, that they should not expose the family as being gluttonous. In the end there is laughter on all faces as the matter is resolved. It must however be emphasised at this juncture, that

Arochukwu customary marriage demands are among the cheapest in Igbo land. Many non-indigenes who come to Arochukwu to marry a wife are amazed at the cheapness and richness of culture of this God's own people.

In Search of the Husband:

When the bottle of three-in-one Scotch whisky has been opened (there is no further requirement for libation since this has been done), the father of the bride is served first as this is his right – it is drink. Then, the bridegroom's father and then the elders of the family of the bride are served, before the elders of the family of the bridegroom.

The bride is then given a tot (shot) of the whisky and she is then told to go out and identify the proposed husband. She is followed by young women and some elderly women and is expected to actually go in search of her proposed husband and even if he is sitting nearby and has already been seen, she must at this stage ignore him and pass by in search and ultimately she comes back to him, kneels down in front of him as a sign of subordination, respect and loyalty. She then sips the drink and hands over the rest to her husband still kneeling. The husband takes the drink from her and gluttonously drinks it dry and then showers her with monetary gifts and is then followed by his father and members of his family. The bride is also given a glass of the palm-wine and this time she merely goes straight to her husband and repeats the same act.

It is appropriate at this stage that although the husband does not go in search of his proposed wife during the course of the 'Mmai-Ajuju' ceremony, yet before the bride comes into the arena, various maidens are paraded around for the bridegroom's father (and not the bridegroom) to identify his proposed daughter-in-law from the bevy of girls. He looks at each girl carefully and rejecting them one after another and in the end when the bride comes in, he identifies her as the chosen one amidst thunderous applause. During the ceremony of 'Mmai-Ajuju', drinks and nourishments are served to the invited guests, the dancers and even the gate-crashers while the official delegation is at this stage restricted to drinks earlier provided by the bride's family since they would be properly entertained after the official ceremony.

STEP FOUR:

'MMAI-IHU ONU AKU' (Wine for the settlement of the bride price):

After the "Mmai-Ajuju" ceremony, the next step in the marriage ceremony is the negotiation of the bride price between the in-laws. It is customary for the son-in-law to produce a full bottle of three-in-one Scotch whisky before the commencement of negotiation. Bride price payment is recognised in all Igbo culture and in some Igbo towns, the price is high and alarming and tends to take account of the beauty of the girl, her level of education etc. In Arochukwu culture, the standard bride price is twelve Nigerian guineas which is now about twenty five Naira forty kobo (N25.40k), since an Aroman does not sell his daughter into slavery under the guise of marriage and in the rare event of dissolution of the marriage, the money would be affordable for refund to the in-laws. However, negotiation nevertheless takes place.

The bride's parents starts by demanding any amount, e.g. twenty thousand Naira or more and the bridegroom's family is expected to bid this down through what may be termed "haggling and bargaining" like any other article of trade. The bridegroom's family may in some cases (particularly if the bridegroom is from another town where bride price is high), be actually ready to pay the sum of twenty thousand Naira or more demanded. At this stage, the final consultation is made by the bride's family and her father or his spokesman (not the general spokesman) usually his first son if he has grown up, will be mandated by her father to announce the amount of bride price. When he gets up, he will salute both his in-laws, family and others by using the expression, "Nde Ogom Mma

Mma Nu" (My in-laws peace be unto you). He thanks his in-laws for their bid and preparedness to pay the huge amount for his daughter. He then narrates her qualities which may include beauty, hard work, chastity, upbringing, education or status in her work place.

He then says that his daughter is really worth more but an Arochukwu man does not sell his daughter and that the Aros are people with tradition and cultures and that he will not be the one to break the custom and tradition and then, he will announce that his in-laws would pay for the marriage of his daughter, twelve guineas (twenty five Naira forty kobo) which is known in Arochukwu custom as "Okwa-isii". At this stage the women folk are in attendance or standing or seating nearby to hear the good news amidst thunderous joy and jubilation by all. The bridegroom's delegation gets up to shake hands with the bride's father and relation and embracing her mother and other elder female relations, in appreciation of the very low bargain and for keeping to tradition. They then offer a bottle of whisky or Schnapps to seal the bargain (Mmai iwu Okwu mmiri). The agreed bride price may be paid on that day or at a later date but by Arochukwu tradition the full amount is never paid because the indebtedness of one in-law to another is perhaps the bond of their relationship.

After the bride price has been negotiated and concluded payment may be made in two separate troughs or metal trays for the bride's father and mother respectively. The father getting double or twice of what is given to the mother. The money is really for the immediate family and is shared out later within the family and if the bride's father gets two Naira, he is lucky. So you can see that apart from other recognised material gifts given to the father and mother, they get little in real terms, of the traditional marriage except the joy of parents in seeing their daughter married. I will discuss or list out the required personal gifts in kind made to each parent later but in the meantime, after "Mmai-Ajuju" and settlement of the bride price, the bride's family will proceed to entertain the bridegroom and his delegation with specially cooked food and other Arochukwu celebration delicacies.

However, in more modern time, the bridegroom is expected to contribute in cash and kind towards the entertainment of all guests although the father-in-law will equally spend money depending on his status, wealth and public standing. These days the families on both sides show off their wealth and capability. However, if the ceremony of "Mmai-Ukwu" will be performed the same day, (whether or not the bride price had been paid), full entertainment and feeding of the bridegroom's delegation will wait and be given after the "Mmai-Ukwu" ceremony (although light refreshment may be given).

Where the "Mmai-Ukwu" ceremony is postponed because of the financial inability of the bridegroom or for other reasons, and in the meantime, the bride becomes pregnant in the hands of the husband due to over-zealousness of either party or marital rascality, the child when born is legitimate, because the pregnancy occurred after consent by her parents in the "Mmai-Ajuju" but the "Mmai-Ukwu" ceremony would not take place until after the child is born. If the "Mmai-Ukwu" ceremony is to take place the same day, the parties proceed immediately to this stage after the settlement of bride price.

STEP FIVE:

MMAI-UKWU (Main Wine)

Mmai-Ukwu is the last formal step in conclusion of the customary marriage rite before full marital status could be conferred on the parties. Whereas, after the "Mmai-Ajuju" ceremony and negotiation and settlement of the bride price, the bride belongs to her husband in equity, "Mmai-Ukwu" celebration on the other hand, clothe the couple legally with the status of husband and wife. It is all drinks and customary gifts to her father and mother which will be discussed later.

Formal requirements of drinks for the main wine ceremony are: six large jars of kegs or pots of palm-wine, (Itotuu isii), six cartons of assorted beer and six crates of assorted soft drinks. Nowadays, because of the acquired taste of the womenfolk on both sides, stout and malt drinks are provided in addition to three packets of cigarettes preferably, Benson and Hedges which replaced players and captain cigarettes, for the young men of the bride's family (Umuokorobia). Out of the six pots (Itotu-Mmai isii) presented by the son-in-law, four are for the father and two are for the mother. The soft drinks are likewise divided between the father and mother in the same ratio of 4 to 2.

However, the bridegroom is required to prop, wedge or support the pots of wine with a bottle of Schnapps without asking, since in Aro custom, hot drink and palm-wine usually complement each other and this in known as, "Nvii-Mmai or Ivii-Mmai). The palm-wine when presented is tested as was done in the case of the palm-wine presented at the "Mmai-Ajuju" (Ile-mmai) to find out the sweetness or otherwise of the wine. As a matter of practice, the wine is declared sour by the testers and the bridegroom is then called upon to improve the test. A token amount was negotiated and agreed to be given. But these days this can run into fifties or hundreds of Naira. Thereafter, the bridegroom and his delegation are fed, entertained as has been said earlier save to say that the bride's father may be required to fill-up i.e. augment the palm-wine (iwuju Mmai) which he does with two jars of palm-wine (about 4 gallons) as sentimentum (Ingegh or Ingheh).

TAKING THE BRIDE AWAY:

After the "Mmai-Ukwu" (main wine) ceremony, the husband may with the consent of his in-laws take his cherished bride away immediately on the principle of "what I have, I hold" and to avoid other suitors of the girl from playing hanky-panky or unacceptable game of eloping with the bride. This was said to have happened some times in the past when in fact a girl was forced by her parents to marry a man she did not love. Of course it was the belief in those days that love starts with marriage and each party will in time learn to love the other spouse. The girl was given little or no choice in the matter, and had to publicly accept to marry a man she does not like. This is no longer the case.

A husband who wants to take his bride away must first offer a keg of palm-wine for the blessing of the bride's womb by her parents – (Mmai ibi afo). Usually however, the taking away takes place on the following day. In both cases, the women, young men and maidens of the girl's family or compound will escort her to her husband's place, carrying various item of household utensils, goods and various clothing and wrappers, domestic animals given to her by her parents, relation and other friends to set up life. This is called (Idu-ulo). Her parents do not escort her to her new home but must give her some days to settle down before visit, to see how she is settling down.

Setting up in life of a girl today does not consist only in the paraphernalia of domestic equipment and its place is now gradually taken by good education (e.g. profession, trade, university degree etc.) of the girl, which enables her to sustain a happy married life. However, well-to-do parents may financially support their daughter in the way that the daughter and husband will prefer. This is a matter between the parties and such support is not put to public glare. Among the less privileged, "Ido-ulo" may be done at any time. Some families leave this until after the birth of the first child of the family where it may be combined with "Uma-nwa" i.e. the celebration of safe delivery.

TRADITIONAL GIFTS BY SON-IN-LAW TO PARENTS-IN-LAW

Father-in-law:

1 flannel jumper (isi-inyinya)
2 fathoms of Indian madras cloth (George cloth)
1 hat (Panama hat or nowadays, bowler hat)
1 walking stick
1 pair of shoes and socks
1 wristwatch (this may not be given)
Ground tobacco (in snuff box or container)

Mother-in-law:

1 good quality blouse
3 fathoms of Indian madras cloth (George material) known as "Oruru na mmakwasi (or Mgbakwasi)"
1 head tie (of good quality)
1 pair of shoes (or slippers)
1 wristwatch (a hand bangle is sufficient)
1 umbrella
1 towel
1 extra large enamel basin
2 bags of edible salt
12 bars of soap
Assorted pomade and talcum powder

The mother-in-law is expected to divide and share out a bag of salt and some of the bar soaps to the family or compound women who assisted her in the arrangement preparation and service during the marriage ceremony.

In addition to the above personal gift items to the parents-in-law, the son-in-law is expected to assist or in some cases fund the general entertainment of his delegation and other guests and would also provide a goat as the case may be. Where the girl's real father is dead, an additional goat will be provided to be killed in his honour. However, rich parents-in-law may waive their right to financial support for the entertainment of guests. How much is given depends on the financial standing of the parties and number of guests expected to be present. There is no fixed amount.

Finally, I must remind you that the customary procedure given above is only satisfied in full by the noble and rich. The poor who make up over seventy percent of Arochukwu population do not and cannot fulfil in full the customary obligations of marriage and whatever is done from the knocking on the door to Mmai-Ajuju will depend on the agreement of both families. However, even the poor try to fulfil the "Mmai-Ukwu", (main wine) with the accompaniment of "Ajuju-Mmai), to prove that there has been marriage and not concubinage. Sometimes, even the bride price is not paid. In such cases, there is no fanfare.

CHAPTER TWO

SETTLEMENT OF MARRIAGE DISPUTES

In the previous chapter, I discussed the steps and procedure to be taken for a full-fledged Arochukwu traditional marriage by the noblemen or rich. I pointed out though that the poor who make up about seventy percent of the population, do not and cannot be expected without assistance of their relatives to meet the ever growing financial burden attendant thereto, due to the escalating costs of the various materials required. So, the poor whittle down the requirements on the principle that "a poor man's goat is his cow". The marriage nevertheless is valid. In this chapter, I will be discussing "settlement of matrimonial disputes" under Arochukwu custom.

Every sphere of human relation has its ups and downs and moments of difficulties, temptation, disagreements and trials and these are also evident in matrimonial relationships. Incompatibility of the parties and other causes including financial may lead to matrimonial ruptures and complete breakdown of the marriage.

In some advanced countries one or both of the parties may seek advice from marriage guidance counsellors at the early stages of disagreement to neutralize the dispute and to save the marriage. However such marriages in most cases are never saved. Under Arochukwu custom, marriage is a family affair (including the extended family) on both sides, a village affair and in some cases a town's affair. Everyone who ought to be present was present during the marriage ceremonies and were witnesses to what took place. So whenever a disagreement arises, the parties would try as much as possible to settle same between themselves without the intervention of any third party, as neither would want to offend all those relations and friends who actively participated in the marriage ceremonies and which may expose the couple or either of them as immature, intolerant of irresponsible.

Parents on both sides particularly the mothers are always ready to advice even when not solicited by either party. They use words and idioms, or narrate from their own experiences of events which tend to unite rather than separate. The young wife is always reminded by her mother not to tarnish the mother's good name, her father's and his family. The husband's mother or father usually does the same with their son. This is an aspect of Arochukwu family relationship which acts as props to support the marriage. In most advanced countries, the son-in-law is always at loggerheads with his mother-in-law because of the attitude of the latter. Most young wives in such advanced countries, on their part, would not want to see their mother-in-law since the marriage was in most cases celebrated in complete independence. There is no such independence under Arochukwu custom as you have read from the previous chapter. Marriage is a family affair no matter the age of the girl to be married. And, any marital action or omission which tends to dislocate the marriage may affect the larger family on both sides.

Not all matrimonial disputes can be settled by the parties. The aggrieved party, if the wife, may seek advice from her husband's mother in the first instance rather than from her own mother. If the aggrieved party is the husband, he would perhaps seek advice from his wife's mother rather than from his own mother who may unwittingly take sides. Usually, most teething marriage problems are settled by the timely intervention of the mother of the persons against whom the complaint was made. However, in more serious cases, the husband he is the aggrieved party, may send his wife down or rusticate her but not to her mother, but to his own parents for a cooling off period and after repentance coupled with the intervention of his parents who do not take any side at this stage, he recalls his wife. Every action or utterance of his parents would be directed towards cementing rather than dislocating the marriage. Sometimes, if the wife was the aggrieved party, she herself would pack some of her belongings and move in with her mother-in-law or his father.

After all it was his father that the young woman was given as wife who in turn presents her to his son. An Aro man would not, no matter how much is to be paid, give away his daughter in marriage, unless the boy's father or other elder male relation, who stands in the place of his father, approaches him to ask for his girl's hand in marriage. It is not money that makes an Aro man but his rich culture and custom (Nwa-Aro icho mkpola icho). He is the person who will have to face his in-laws, he is the person to take the blame and be answerable should anything happen to the young woman. He will send for his son and will use his good offices to resolve the conflict. He does not take sides with either party at this stage, but would dish out blames as he sees fit. And, no husband would want to create such opportunity to be castigated and this tends to keep the parties in the path of marriage righteousness.

Sometimes, it does happen that either party has exhausted mediatory role of the husband's parents without change of heart by the offending party, the wife, if she is the aggrieved party would take some of her belongings and return to her parents. This is a serious matter, which has to be handled with care and tact. Her father, on seeing her and after hearing her grievance would if he finds her complaint frivolous in the sense that her husband has a right to do what he had done e.g. taking an "Uzi" (a sort of concubine who is not resident) will take her back to her husband and try to iron out their differences.

If however, the daughter was compelled to flee the husband's house due to persistent beating, brutality, starvation or by persistent disparaging remarks being made of her parents by the husband without abatement, her father will in the meantime, send a message to his in-law the husband's father, to inform him that his wife (daughter) has come back to his house.

On receipt of the message above, the father-in-law will send back message that he would come to see him on a certain day. In the meantime, he will send for his son to find out what the problem was which led to the wife fleeing his house. Perhaps they may not be unconnected with problems which he had mediated on in the past. After hearing his side of the dispute, as an Aro man, he would know whether his son was wrong or that the young wife was being unreasonable. If he is of the view that his son was wrong, he will know how to approach his in-laws on the date of his visit, whilst in the meantime, thoroughly castigating his son for letting him down and exposing him and his family to ridicule, disgrace, contempt and odium in Arochukwu town. He will in advance, after consultation with his family, determine what would be done to appease his in-laws and to take back his wife (son's wife).

MATRIMONIAL CONCILIATION & APPEASEMNT

On the appointed day usually on "Eke", "Orie" or "Afor" (Avor)" market day, the husband's father will visit his in-laws, accompanied by some members of his family versed in Arochukwu custom. After exchange of pleasantries, they are offered kola-nuts, his in-law would pour libation with any hot drink available in his house (but usually Schnapps or Scotch whisky) or palm wine. After the visiting party have settled down, the matter is introduced. Sometimes, it is he husband's father who tell his in-laws that he has come because of his message that his wife (daughter-in-law) has returned to the in-laws' house and that he has come to find out the reason she gave for deserting her husband. Although, he knows the reason or probable reason, yet he would not prompt the issue until after the woman's grievance has been narrated by her father. Sometimes, it would be necessary to send for both wife and husband to hear their first-hand account of the quarrel which led to his wife deserting him. If the husband is not readily available, the conciliation process would be adjourned to another date, when he is expected to attend.

On the resumed hearing, the wife and husband would in turn narrate their story and each person is then questioned by the other spouse or any of the parties present including their parents. In the end, the husband and wife are sent out for the deliberation of the joint family. Sometimes, either group of the families may request to be allowed to go outside for private consultation, called in Arochukwu dialect, "Igba-izu or Ichi-ikpu"

RULING (DECISION)

On the return of the family that went outside, they would announce to the other side their proposal for amicable settlement. If this is agreed upon by all parties, and if the husband is found to be the guilty party, his own father will be mandated to announce the ruling or decision of the joint family to his own son so that it carries weight and create remorse. He would be told to do certain things or to refrain from doing certain things. He is also told what to do to appease his wife and her father respectively in order to take her back. The wife will not be around when this sentence as it were, is passed on her husband, so as not to deride him in the presence of his wife and thereby unwittingly diminishing his authority in his own house. The whole procedure is conciliatory and not punishment. He would be thoroughly reprimanded.

When the wife is invited in, it is necessary for her father to give her an indication that everything has been settled and that the husband has promised to treat her better. She would not be told the imposition meted on her husband and would be advised to follow her husband home or that he would come (after of course he has appeased his father-in-law and his own father) to take back his wife. What other tangible things like clothing etc. which he has been asked to purchase for his wife will be given to her when she has returned home as a welcome present. Sometimes, a general fine is imposed on him for the benefit of the joint families, in the nature of "ngwa-ato or ngwa-isii" (not intended to be discussed in the present work).

If however the wife was wrong in deserting her husband or perhaps in situations, where her husband sent her away for an alleged matrimonial offence which is not serious, she will be reprimanded by her own father for disgracing him and his family and exposing them to ridicule, contempt, and odium. He will call her a bad daughter and would tell her that she does not resemble her mother in manners at all. She is then told what to do or refrain from doing to appease her husband and her father-in-law. She will finally kneel down before her father and father-in-law in turn and beg for mercy. Thereafter, the women usually, her mother, and other elder women of her family will take her out. In the olden days, she would be crying as a way of showing her remorse when escorted out of the venue.

DIVORCE (ACHOKWAM)

Divorce as we know it today, was rare or non-existent in Arochukwu custom but separation whether temporary or permanent was then the method of disengagement from marital cohabitation, where a serious marital offence has been committed by either spouse - on the part of the wife, adultery, unmitigated fighting, public quarrels, disobedience, fraud, flippancy or lacking of concealment of secrets etc. On the husband's part, brutality, neglect, drunkenness, social disgrace, etc. but never adultery since the society at the time was basically polygamous, except for people married in the Church or Marriage Registry under the Marriage Act, when adultery by either spouse could lead to the breakdown and dissolution of the marriage unless condoned by the other spouse. Even in Arochukwu culture, adultery by the wife may not automatically lead to the dissolution of marriage if her husband forgives her and she appeases his kitchen by the ceremony of "Igwa-ekwu" and vows to sin no more.

Marriage offences no matter how grave may still be conciliated upon either by the families, compound, kindred or the Eze Aro i.e., the Paramount Ruler of Arochukwu. But, when every mediatory role has been explored by either party to no avail, then the marriage has broken down irretrievably and there would be temporary or permanent separation or perhaps divorce (Achokwam).

The mere fact that a man sends his wife out of his house, or a woman says that she will no longer be married to her husband does not bring about divorce or "Achokwam", unless the bride price on her head is refunded to her husband by her parents. If the bride price is not refunded, the parties may still resume co-habitation after certain ceremonies of appeasement which may include oath taking ("ita arunsi"). If the bride price is not refunded, any children born by her out of wedlock belong to her husband. However, if her husband, in uncontrollable fury or rage, throws her out from his house with her belongings on an "Nkwo market day", the marriage has broken down irretrievably and her father will under no circumstance allow her to go back to the husband as this is a grave insult to him and his family. This does not stop the wife going back to her husband but in such event, she will be disinherited by her father.

THE CUSTOMARY COURT:

After the Arochukwu conquest of 1901 to 1902, the British Colonial Administrators set up a Customary Court in Arochukwu. This court was rarely used. However, the Nigerian Constitution has entrenched the institution of Customary Court which now has power among other things to determine issues of breakdown of customary marriage and dissolution of same. It has no power however, in determining issues connected with marriage under the Marriage Act (Church and registry marriage). The Aros did not trust any court whether civil or customary for the settlement of disputes as they looked on such set-up as an unnecessary interference with their ability to resolve issues affecting them. Remember, that Arochukwu was the land of Long Juju which had settled disputes throughout Igboland.

Finally, from the discussion above, the reader would have found out why there are little or no divorces by Arochukwu people. The known cases of divorce involving an Arochukwu person (man or woman) have been with outside marriages, i.e. a marriage between an Aro man with non-Aros because there may not be similar procedures detached from personal sentiments through which the marriage could be saved. On the other hand, Arochukwu Customary Marriages have built-in procedures for conciliation mediation and separation.

CHAPTER THREE

"UZISHIP IN AROCHUKWU"

The institution of "Uziship" or "Uzi" in Arochukwu is as old as Arochukwu history. Uzi is a relationship whereby a married man or a middle aged or fully grown man who is either a bachelor or a widower, will befriend a middle aged but single woman, a widow or fully grown but unmarried woman (Senior Miss) that both man and woman are locked-up in romance and love in a relationship short of marriage. This relationship is open and public and well accepted by Arochukwu culture. The man doing for the woman most or all a husband should in those days do for a woman such as mending the thatched roof of her house, cutting or hiring people to cut the bush for her for farming and generally supporting her financially and morally.

The Uzi culture was distinguished from prostitution of both young women, married or other women. Whereas Uziship was accepted, prostitution by women i.e., flirting from one man to another was objectionable. Uziship was open and public, whereas prostitution was secretly performed under various clandestine arrangements and when discovered, incurred the displeasure of the village or town.

For example, prostitution or sexual intimacy between a woman and another man was in Arochukwu history objectionable and is regarded a heinous crime for which the death penalty could in ancient times be imposed on the erring woman and brings about feud between the husband and the other person or that person's family. In more modern times, if the woman confesses and the husband still loves his wife, the woman would be ordered by the community to appease her husband's kitchen before the husband could be expected to eat what is cooked by her. This might involve killing a goat or other animal, hot drink, palm wine, Kolanuts, etc. according to the tradition of Arochukwu. The elderly men and women from both sides of the family are in attendance to see that justice is done and that the woman was not punished for an offence she has not committed. Usually, if her guilt is proven, even her parents will reprimand her and side with the husband. The Aro man of old did not condone evil deeds – they stood for the truth no matter whose ox is gored. The ceremony of appeasing the husband's kitchen is called, "Igwa-ekwu". This is still practiced today but, to a lesser extent. Where the married woman is suspected but denies ever having an extra-marital affair, it was usual practice for her to swear to the native oath (Ita-arunsi).

Prostitution by a young unmarried woman however, although repugnant to the social decency was not a taboo (tabu) although it had its own consequences. Such a girl may never find a reputable husband in Arochukwu as she will not be put in the fattening room for the purpose of dancing at the Eke-Ekpe Day during the New Yam Festival (Ikeji) which was supposedly meant for virgins and was also the pride of her parents – particularly her mother. In most recent past, other girls, perhaps, whose own guilt have not surfaced will compose and sing derogatory songs about her. This sometimes led to public accusations by both sides of each other's hidden frolics with men in the maiden dance (Ojojo).

Sometimes, there were brutal fights among the girls because of the unrestrained public verbal attacks through "Ojojo songs" on the reputation and character of young women innocent or otherwise. Because of modernism, civilization or the so-called Western education, these one-time entrenched moral standards of young women are no longer maintained to their ancient level. The situation has been made worse by the affliction of economic hardship on parents and children alike which, makes some parents to ignore the tradition of the past because of the quest for or greed for money. These unwholesome relationships although, part of the modern society in Nigeria (Arochukwu inclusive), are not the institution of Uziship as known to the Aro man.

The Uzi was highly respected in Arochukwu tradition and as I said earlier was open and public. The wife of the house knew her husband's Uzi and both the wife and the Uzi accepted each other's position with respect and there was no antagonism of one by the other. The Uzi never exceeds her bounds and was, welcomed into the family. Even the children of the family treated her with respect. The woman Uzi has only one male Uzi at a time and the relationship will span over a number of years. Sometimes, children may be born out of the relationship and although by Arochukwu customary law or tradition, the children are not legally the man's children, yet he is obliged to look after them but not as he would have, if they were his children born in wedlock. The children do not take his name as surname although they look up to him as papa (father). However, they interact with other children of the family. I must hasten to say, that Arochukwu Customary Law has not developed very much in the area of children born out of wedlock unlike the Yoruba Land, where such children if accepted by their father, have the same rights as children born in wedlock.

Uziship is a real and virile institution. And, not merely because a man and woman (even married people) call themselves "Uzi" that they are regarded as Uzi. This is a joke – Uzi which people may call themselves when they have mutual respect for each other and share some jokes unrelated to sexual relationship. This is not the Uziship which I am discussing with you. Uziship confers status, whereas other clandestine relationships do not. In Arochukwu of old (and in some instances even today) when a daughter has passed marriageable age the parents will call together the family and relations and after discussing her position with them a ceremony or ritual will be performed called "Iruwe-akuu" whereby the elder women of the family or compound will dress her up by tying around their waist George-cloth (Indian Madras cloth) and she is then given the status of a married woman, who was free to choose her Uzi and subsequently will introduce him to the family. The woman and her children are regarded as legitimate children of her father and no one raises eyebrow in her relationship with men. Sometimes, some fathers, who have no sons will deliberately induct a loved daughter, usually the first daughter (Ada) in the ceremony of "Iruwe-akuu", and thereby confers on her a status in the family and accepts her children as his legitimate children. Officially she takes on an Uzi. So you can see why the institution tradition or culture of Uziship is different from other acts of promiscuity of infidelity or promiscuity since the trade of prostitution is as old as the Bible – but this is not Uziship as practiced by the Aros of old. Today people in order to clothe their clandestine relationships with respectability refer to such relationship as Uziship or Uzi – it is not.

CONCLUSION

Finally, it would have occurred to the reader that I have been discussing women infidelity and not that of the men. In Arochukwu of old as in most African societies, polygamy was largely practised, hence you have heard of people saying that their grand-parents had several wives at a time. Thus, most large families in Arochukwu today are as a result of this. Polygamy is no longer widely practised anymore because of the Law (The Marriage Act), which has deterred people from marrying many wives, as well as harsh economic realities.

The Late Dr T.O. Elias, when he was the Chief Justice of Nigeria was quoted as saying that if the Law of Bigamy was rigidly enforced in Nigeria, most Nigerian men who married in the Church or Registry (monogamous marriages) will go to prison because bigamy is a crime. A visit to some states in Nigeria will confirm that the then Chief Justice was speaking the truth.

Bigamy is rarely practiced by the Aro man due to the advent of Christianity which preaches monogamy and I am not aware of any reported case. Some believe that the institution of Uziship also played a part in cushioning-off the desire to commit bigamy. However, such Uziship or extra-marital relationship may lead to divorce if the marriage has broken down irretrievably because of same. Some Aro men who have not married in their church believe they still retain their right to polygamous marriage even when not exercised. For such people, Uziship may hold an attraction.

However, "Uziship" today is an adulterated culture providing an umbrella for all sorts of surreptitious relationships where the women involved do not gain the same reputable status as existed in the olden days. Uziship was an open and public relationship accepted by the community which conferred respectability and status on the woman. This is not to say that the other forms of marital infidelity promiscuity or rascality were not present, operating side by side with the institution of Uziship. However everyone knew the distinction between them.

GEORGE M. ONWUCHEKWA ESQ
(Iyiukwu-Aro)

AROCHUKWU
(LAND OF MY BIRTH)

DEDICATION

Dedicated to AROCHUKWU YOUTHS
OF YESTERYEARS OF TODAY AND
OF TOMORROW

By George M. Onwuchekwa Esq.

(Iyiukwu-Aro)

TABLE OF CONTENTS

PREFACE

CHAPTER ONE

Introduction

CHAPTER TWO

Making of the Aroman (Aroversity)

CHAPTER THREE

(i) Western Education
(ii) Early Arochukwu Educated Men
(iii) Sports and Sporting Activities
(iv) Politics
(v) Healthcare

CHAPTER FOUR

(i) Arochukwu Town
(ii) Barracks (Baraki)
(iii) Aggrey Memorial College
(iv) Slessor
(v) Amanagwu Square
(vi) Iyiukwu Obinkita
(vii) Mgbala-Ekpe Amanagwu
(viii) Ujari Village
(ix) Ulonta Ndi-Okoroji
(x) Ibom Village
(xi) Aburuma Ibom
(xii) Eze Aro's Palace
(xiii) Africa Road
(xiv) Amaikpe Square: Obinkita Village
(xv) Ikeji Festival

CHAPTER FIVE

(i) Eke-Ekpe Day
(ii) Amaikpe Square as Market
(iii) Amaoba Village & Ngeleokwo
(iv) Arochukwu Mission School & Church
(v) Eke-Ukwu Market
(vi) Atani Village and other Villages

CHAPTER SIX

(i) Arochukwu Ancient Storey Houses
(ii) The Tunnel Bridge and the Legend of botched Railway line
(iii) Conclusion

PREFACE

I have been motivated to write this book, because of the unusual inquiries which I receive from Arochukwu men and women who ought to know but who exhibit utter ignorance about some of the various landmarks depicting Arochukwu history and social heritage. I also wish to give a sustained encouragement to knowledgeable Arochukwu men and women versed in Arochukwu history, anthropology, progenitors and rich cultural and social heritage in the hope that they will put their knowledge on paper for posterity instead of departing this God-given world with that knowledge and unwittingly truncating whatever knowledge the outside world has about God's own people – "Umu-Chukwu" or "Arochukwu". Save for few exceptions, e.g. under the Official Secrets Acts, grounds of security or established custom, the recipient or a person endowed with knowledge, holds that knowledge on sacred trust to disseminate same for the benefit of humanity. Knowledge is not private property. Therefore, the motive of my second coming is not financial, since all the copies of my first pamphlet "AROCHUKWU MARRIAGE CUSTOM" were given away free of charge – all costs of production borne by me.

The present book is not a book on Arochukwu history neither is it a geography book of Arochukwu. It is not essentially a treatment of its customs and traditions nor of its supremacy or hegemony over other Igbo towns. From its very limited scope, it is not intended to be my autobiography, but merely my childhood reflections and reminiscences of people and places including events and things around me at the time of my early development at Arochukwu Town. The period covered is mainly between 1934 and 1950 although casual reference is made of succeeding years.

As most of the work is devoted to my childhood experiences, it is possible some of the events and things "which seemed to seem were not what they seemed." I should be forgiven for any exaggeration of events. However, at three score years (as at the time of writing in 1994), I am still convinced that my early perceptions were correct. After all, I knew the difference between Giant Alakuku said to be an Arochukwu man, whom I saw, and other homosapiens.

Most Aro-Children of my generation would have passed through similar tutelage and for the silent majority, "I am writing for you." The book may be regarded as a study of the sociological aspect of the legendary "Aroman", what makes the Aroman tick. And, no matter from what perspective that one looks at the book, it is bound to give one an incisive appreciation of the Aro-man – a spiritual nourishment, and excite your inner feeling of spiritual and cultural rebirth.

I am grateful to all the departed Arochukwu sages to whom I carried errands or messages from my late father among whom were the late Dr Alvan Ikoku; the late Mazi Kanu Oji (the Eze Aro); the late Mazi Anicho Anyakaoha; the late Mazi Obasi Onwuchekwa; the late Mazi Inyamah Ukwuivi; the late Mazi Okereke Ojiugwo; the late Mazi Ogbonnaya Anicho (Eze Ogo Obinkita); the late Teacher Emmanuel Oti; the late T.K. Utchey, and the late Mazi S.O. Nwangoro. Above all, I am indeed indebted to my father the late Teacher Moses Onwuchekwa who exposed me very early to Aroversity – (Arochukwu University of Understanding), by trying me on delicate errands to the above sages in spite of my trembling lips and wobbling knees coupled with my fidgeting hands, induced by intense fear.

I make bold to say that mistakes, misrepresentations, and distortions of facts (if any) are entirely mine of which I accept full responsibility and are in no way attributable to my childhood contact with these departed progenitors of Arochukwu. Lastly, I am grateful to my dear wife Mary Magdalene for her encouragement and insistence that I should put my recollections on paper and also for proof-reading the book. Lastly, I am grateful to my secretary Miss Mary Nosakhare for typing this work.

George Moses Onwuchekwa Esq (Iyiukwu-Aro)

Monday 16 May 1994

Chapter One

INTRODUCTION

Three score years ago (in Onwuchekwa family), Obinkita Village in the ancient town of Arochukwu – the land of the proverbial "Long-juju" or ibinukpabi, a son was born to Teacher Moses Onwuchekwa and his wife Madam Grace Mgbokwo Onwuchekwa. That son is me. I was the second son of my parents and their third child. Large families were in vogue at the time.my parents had altogether eight children, four males and four females.

1934, the year of my birth, was still during the great economic and financial depression which afflicted the world (including Nigeria) after the 1st World War from the late nineteen twenties to early nineteen thirties. From around 1939, when my reasons germinated, Arochukwu town was still volatile; slave trade was still clandestinely carried on in spite of the fact that a white District Officer and white missionaries were resident at Arochukwu with the paraphernalia and retinue of British colonial authority. The period however, could not be described as part of the dark ages of Arochukwu history and hegemony, and in spite of the great depression when items of human comfort were scarce or expensive, it was a period of revival of Arochukwu art, culture, discipline and reluctant acceptance of the white man's education alongside Arochukwu educated persons before the nineteen thirties, these could be counted by the fingers – not until the establishment of Aggrey Memorial College by late Dr Alvan Ikoku that there was a surge in the number of Arochukwu college attendance.

I could not have missed the feelings and the expectations of the time together with the very rigid parental regimentation. In those days, children even from birth were tutored to understand their environment, its people, culture and places including its taboos – whether or not they could, because of their tender ages understand what was being hammered into their tender brains. Regular doses of instructions continued unabated. Every instruction of an elder was punctuated with stories of witches, spirits, demons, head-hunters, rituals, shrines, forefathers (ndichie), sacrifices, oaths taking (arunsi) and juju. After all, Arochukwu is the land of the infamous Long-juju (Ibinukpabi).

The intelligence of the Aro-man was a matter of common knowledge. Unintelligence was regarded as an anathema and a curse of the gods as punishment for imaginary offence committed by a person in previous world before death and reincarnation. For example, at each exhibition of minor aberration by a young man or woman the question was rightly put to him as to whether in reality, he or she was an Arochukwu child (i-bukwa nwa Aro). Such expression of resentment towards ignorance, stupidity or unintelligence was worse than corporal punishment which was promptly and regularly administered to young persons with reckless abandon. "Spare the rod and spoil the child" my father would say.

My parents being Christians (Church of Scotland Mission now the Presbyterian Church), my father both a school teacher and Church elder, did not suffocate me with fairy tales; yet their watch-words were discipline, obedience, respect for elders, respect for the custom of the land, except where the custom is flagrantly in conflict with Christian tenets, then such custom must not be obeyed but should be corrected if one can. My father respected culture and tradition and poured libation for the appeasement of the spirits of departed parents and relations and saw nothing wrong about it. He welcomed the Ekpo masquerade to his premises to dance for him. He liked the dance and culture but not their rituals. He attended the Eke-Ekpe celebration during yam festivals and took us along to watch the dancers and masquerades and regarded these as part of our culture, our history and our social heritage. He did not however indulge in festishness. These he regarded as against Christian tenets.

Obedience to the head of family was expected. The head of family may not even be the parents of the young person, but are other senior relations of the overall family – particularly in a polygamous community, which most Arochukwu families belonged at the time. The position of the head of the family in Arochukwu was similar to the position of the Roman paterfamilias. The head of the family exerted much influence in the upbringing of the children. The family included not only the children of a father or descendants or near relations of the head of the family, but servants and in some cases liberated slaves who had chosen to stay with the family. After the world-wide abolition of slave trade, slaves who had nowhere to go, or who were well treated by their former owners remained in the families, became part of it and in some cases were assimilated. Those slaves that were too eager to grab their freedom found themselves enslaved again elsewhere as slavery was still surreptitiously carried on. I saw many slaves in Arochukwu and one or two were still living in my family compound. Therefore, apart from the circumstances of their birth, or coming into a particular family, they were for all intents and purposes, members of the larger family.

At the period under review, there was little distinction between a brother, cousin etc. Every young person in the larger family was just "brother" or "sister". The elder ones were called "de-de or dee" for the males or "daa" for the females. The very old male family relations were called "Mazi" or "Nna" (father). These words were used as prefix before the name of the particular elder relations. It was an act of gross indiscipline to call an elder by his name without the appropriate prefix.

A child's education started from the family. There he was taught (if his parents are knowledgeable) about Arochukwu, the likes and taboos. The period of my childhood was a period of folklores, fables, moonlight plays (Egwu-Onwa), ballards, dances, and keen observation. Children were taught to observe the movement of the eyes, hands and body, the art of getting up and sitting down as messages were transmitted through all these movements – particularly warning of danger. Nowadays the rotation or twinkling of an eye to a child will meet an immediate rude response or embarrassment from the child who would probably question the parent loudly what is wrong with his or her eye and why he or she is twinkling their eye. This is in complete ignorance or lack of appreciation of signals transmitted by the eye or other bodily movement.

In Arochukwu of my childhood, a child or young person never questions his parents in the public. In private the question would be addressed to a parent or elder in such a way to show that no offence was intended. Most often, the question was instead put to an immediate elder relation to find out reasons for certain behaviours. Mothers are more sympathetic than fathers. To the father, a child is only seen but must not be heard. In my own case, I had a very understanding father – understanding because he was a teacher but answers were not given to me freely until I was castigated for my lack of perception and ignorance which had no room under our roof. I was reminded of how I fumbled at previous occasions. Little did I know I was undergoing a pupillage in my first classes of "Aroversity" or Arochukwu University of Understanding.

Chapter Two

MAKING OF THE ARO-MAN (AROVERSITY)

As part of a child's traditional education, team spirit in him was encouraged and developed and also his respect for hierarchical order of birth. He was assigned under an elder relative in the company of his peer group to perform some tasks e.g. fetching water from the stream, entering the forest to gather firewood for cooking, going to the farm to assist the parents or other elder family relations. During these activities, which were in those days not easy, as every step was fraught with danger, wild animals like leopards, boa constrictor, cobra, chimpanzees and even gorillas and buffalo still inhabited the various outskirts of Arochukwu. The areas in Arochukwu today which are adorned with state of the art dream houses depicting the lifestyle of rich and famous, were once inhabited by these wild animals. With the exception of the gorilla, I saw all the above animals and creatures in the wild.

It would have been unimaginable in those days to think of people trying to settle in the various wooded, and in those days regarded as out of the way, forests, some of which were closely associated with demons, etc. Even hunters came back home to tell a tale of woe and of their exploits and supernatural powers over the demons, and ghosts. The Arochukwu of my childhood was of course a different age and a different place. Thus children were taught basic natural first aid techniques and of self-preservation and defence. Self-defence only as a last resort – for example snakes and leopards could be detected by their different bodily odour. The sharpness of the odour will indicate the nearness or otherwise of the creature from the individual. Eyes were trained to be sharp in the detection at first glance of unusual movements of people, leaves, objects and things. Quick escape techniques were taught in addition to the use of certain leaves/herbs and plants with pungent smell which were quickly gathered, squeezed and applied to the body to ward off the intruder.

Various edible wild fruits were on a forest expedition gathered and taken home by the children in addition to firewood and other edible vegetables (Okazi) not because fruits were not available at home but for variety. Arochukwu in those days was richly endowed with fruits. Where the children were not sure of the quality or toxicity of particular well-ripened invitingly ready-for-eating fruits, they will simply take samples home for proper identification by their parents.

Fruits which were commonly found in Arochukwu woods at that time were "ubune" (a sort of wild grape-like clustered fruit), "ukwubia", "ichaara", "kpikirikpi", wild mangoes, "utu", "Udara", wild pineapples – in the sparsely wooded lands between Obinkita Village and Utugugwu Village all the way to the back of Hugh Goldie College. Domesticated fruits were oranges, pawpaw (called mgbimgbi), mangoes, "ntum" (a ripe fruit which is not delicious by itself but which after eating makes other sour fruits like lime or even palm wine delicious. Ntum was found mostly in Ugbo village and some other villages; "ochicha", "ube" (black plum-like fruit or pear which when soft – either naturally, by roasting or boiling was used in eating corn), avocado, banana, and guava. Nuts and spices gathered in the wild included "evure", "uziza", "akpi" – said to drive away witches, "ugba" (oil bean) a popular delicacy in Igboland, "uda". Wild vegetables were "okazi", "uziza – leaves", "utazi", "nturukpa", "ataama" etc.

I always enjoyed the outing into the forests with my peer group, although I was not always allowed to go, because at the time I was considered too young to cope with the hazards or dangers of the forest until I was ten years of age. Rather, I always accompanied my father by carrying his umbrella or other items wherever he went, whilst he carried his walking stick, properly attired in Indian Madras loin-cloth (George material) with a well-tailored jumper on top with a suitable hat. When I was twelve years of age, I was sent to live with my maternal uncle who was a teacher at "Amaodu" in "Ututu" a nearby town which is only a distance of about three miles from my home. Here, I was seriously subjected to the rigours of involuntary service. However, with my Arochukwu natural intelligence and home training, I soon became a leader of other house servants in the school compound where we lived and in no time, I became a forest guide.

"Ututu Town" being of traditional farmers in the mid-nineteen forties was not as developed as the town of Arochukwu. It had hitherto unexplored and un-exploited natural forests and wooded terrain. After about two years sojourn at Ututu Town, I was recalled home by my father (a headmaster of schools). Little did I know, at the time, that being sent away to stay with my uncle was a necessary part of my training and education. It was the practice in those days for children to stay for a few years with a trusted relation or family friend (if one could be found). My father, being a well to do person in his days and prominent in school, church and society, had at one time or another, during the same period that I was sent away, not less than ten young men and women who were children of friends and relations staying with him and to whom he stood in loco-parentis; yet he found the need to send me to acquire knowledge and experience elsewhere. He was an affluent person with a storey house built in the nineteen twenties. The ancient building is still standing till this day – so it was not because of want of funds that compelled him to send me to my uncle but love. I owe much in my life today to this training.

When I eventually returned home, to continue my formal school education after my brief sojourn, little did I know that I was then ready to commence the next stage of my Aroversity (University of Understanding). Although I always accompanied him to see various people and places, this time, I was more visible in his company and had things explained to me. I held his umbrella, leather bag containing kolanut, documents and writing materials, or held anything else I was given to hold, during our various outings. I followed him to important meetings both religious and secular as his valet (inya-akpa), to burials, marriages, and disputes settlement meetings. He exposed me to his friends and told me of the idiosyncrasies of others.

For example, he told me before we set off on my first visit with him to the late Dr Alvan Ikoku, that he Dr Ikoku was the most intelligent Aroman alive. I was told to listen carefully to whatever he said because his words were always loaded with meaning, idioms and wisdom. It was on that occasion that I heard late Dr Ikoku saying during their discussion about an individual, known to both of them that "Nwa achoghi ka nne na nna ziya ihe, eluwa ga ezi ya ihe" (meaning a child who does not want the training of the mother and father will be taught the hard way by the world). My father turned his eyes on me and I understood. On our getting to Aggrey Memorial College, Late Dr Ikoku was very happy to see my father and very soon, both masters of Arochukwu custom were locked in idioms and riddles, both in the English Language and in my native tongue – and I was completely lost.

Although late Dr Ikoku turned his eyes once or twice towards me, he did not say anything to me during the tête-à-tête. However, as we were about to leave, he tapped me by the shoulder and looking at my father he said "Moses you have a very attentive son." This was perhaps because I was not at once, (even though I was protesting inside) distracted by the football game that was going on in the field opposite the house to which my father jokingly replied "Ani odo anagi amu nkakwu" meaning literally a good tree does not bear bad fruit. The happiness of my father with me on our way home was a marked difference from his attitude the previous day when I escaped from the venue of a very important meeting at Atani Village, to join other children to play "koso" game and "otikpaa" outside. My punishment was a sufficient deterrent for repeat performance in a short space of time.

As was said earlier, my father would expose me to people and places at Arochukwu town and would frequently send me on important errands and, it was not long, that I was well known by sight, by prominent elder citizens of various villages. Some of the elders that I came in contact by the fact of being my father's errand boys were: late Mazi Kanu Oji (the Eze Aro); late Dr Alvan Ikoku; late Mazi Anicho Anyakaoha of Amankwu Village, late Mazi Inyama Ukwuivi of Ibom Village, late teacher Jack Ogbonnaya of Ibom Village who was my father's best man at his church wedding with my mother in 1927; late Elder udo Okoroafor of Ugbo Village; late Mazi Anicho the Eze-Ogo Obinkita; late Mazi Okereke the father of Mazi Kanu Okereke of Amanagwu Village; late Mazi T.K. Utchey his classmate at Hope Waddell Calabar; late Mazi T.E. Ijomah of Amangwu Village; late Madam Rebecca James the matron of Slessor School and late headmaster Emmanuel Oti of "Hope Villa" Ibom.

Arochukwu Town in the period from 1934 up to and including 1950, was a town of mystical or supposed mystical powers, or rainmakers, taboos, stories of witches and wizards, private gods and deities and progenitors (ndichie). Any action or event that could not be explained was a visitation of the forefathers. For example, the total eclipse of the sun in 1947 was wrongly attributed to some evil spirits. Some people were quick to point out that it was caused by one obnoxious rainmaker who was not paid all his fees for services rendered at a public celebration. These fairy-tales and superstitions were prevalent in spite of the strong inroads made by the presence of white missionaries notably the Church of Scotland Mission which was firmly established in Slessor, Hugh Goldie, and at the mission school Obinkita all with European missionaries in situ. Their old wooden or half-wooden elevated bungalows or storey houses can still be seen in these locations as symbols of our progressive past. The seat of the colonial government with a white district officer or white assistant district officer occupying also a wooden elevated bungalow with his retinue of command had been firmly established in Arochukwu and yet Arochukwu feudal tendencies and beliefs continued unabated. After all Arochukwu was the land of the mystical Long-Juju.

Behind the façade of mysticism, Arochukwu of the period of my childhood was a town of honesty, dignity, integrity, fairness, truth, love, communal effort, self-respect, culture, art, music and above all discipline. For example, a man will never deny obligation or indebtedness to his fellow citizen although there was present inability to pay. He will in fact on his death-bed, instruct his sons to settle such debt or handover certain parcels of land given to him by way of pledge to their rightful owners once the loan was repaid – this was in spite of the fact that such obligations were never reduced into writing. Stealing was rare and robbery was non-existent. If a person stole, his family will not protect him but will in fact expose him to the community as to maintain the good name of the family. A necklace or chain of empty snail shells was hung on the neck of the thief and he was publicly paraded and disgraced to deter others.

The next stage of a young man's Aroversity was his exposure to his village. This would include perhaps his initiation into the main traditional institution of "ekpe–na–mboko", although some children were initiated so young and before they could understand what it was all about – not unlike infant baptism. Though initiation was in the institution of his own village, yet initiation was recognised and respected throughout the entire town and in all towns in what is now Cross River, Abia and Akwa Ibom States. Initiation attracted respect, security, and other privileges. Whether or not initiated, a young person was encouraged by his family to take more active part in village activities with his age-group and if he makes his mark or shows promises of leadership, he will start gradually easing his foot slowly into Arochukwu Town gatherings and public affairs.

At the Arochukwu level, he is very conscious of his speech, and behaviour – weighing every word, expression or idiom carefully before utterance, using his eyes, and listening carefully and learning from others. An Aro-man does not dabble into a discussion until he understands so to say "the head and tail" of the matter being discussed; "anagi abu okwu ubu" (one does not scramble at discussions). He would tap on his resource of earlier training and is eager to learn more since

Aroversity is a life time commitment and continuing process. When his views (and not his money or wealth) become acceptable in Arochukwu important gathering or meeting, he would unknowingly have earned his degree and has become an Aro-man, and is then ready to take on all and sundry no matter from which part of the globe or colour or colour of the skin in the battle of wits, and diplomacy.

Aroversity (Arochukwu University of Understanding – "U.U"), is not a building or comprising of classrooms, tables, benches and chairs. It does not consist of formal lectures, books and writings. It is the amalgam or totality of a child's education of his environment, people and places from his birth, through manhood and until death. A successful graduand of Aroversity (the Aro-man or Aro-son) is different from every male son born of Arochukwu parents. To naïve categories of Aro-man, I ask "Ibukwa Nwa-Aro" and "imakwara anya elere-ele na anya aroro aro." A real Aro son understands Aro tradition and custom (including the breaking or sharing of Kola-nuts and of serving wine and hot drinks at gatherings) he behaves himself in public – particularly in the presence of non-Aros. He is not gluttonous in public and suppresses hunger and holds himself with dignified composure.

When I was young (about ten years of age) my parents or either of them will take me and sometimes with one or more of my brothers and sisters to visit friends and relations – perhaps, after a Sunday's church service, which in those days lasted more than two hours and I would have become so famished and thirsty. In our host's house, food and other delicacies were laid before us. We will pass quick glances at each other and at our parents without giving away our motive or raising suspicion. Our parents' eyes even though not blinking, pass on the message whether or not we were to savour the dainty dishes. If we interpreted our parent's look to mean "don't touch it", no matter the open persuasion of our parents and the host, we will not eat or drink anything.

I remember an event on one occasion, when I attended a funeral church service with my father. After the burial, it was the tradition and still is the tradition that guests are entertained in groups depending on their status or relationship. I was in the same room with my father, where distinguished (although not me) guests were seated for entertainment. A man I had seen many times before gave me a chunky piece of meat from his plate. I quickly feigned clumsiness and deliberately dropped the piece of meat near a dog which was lurking nearby, and it quickly carried it away. One could see the frustration and anger of the person who gave me the meat. My father stood up from his seat and slapped me (even though it did not hurt much like his usual), calling me degrading names and ordering me to go home straight as I was a disappointment. I ran out in shame and went home as ordered. When my father returned, he called me, but I was still terrified, suspecting additional punishment. He did not reproach me, instead informed my mother, brothers and sisters how savoir-faire I was and invited me to eat with him from the same plate that evening – a rare privilege in those days. He gave me a piece of meat more chunky than the one I had thrown to the dog. In addition I was showered with encomium.

These days, one is horrified to numbness when one sees some children – even children of the educated and well to do, scrambling for biscuits, food and soft drinks in a house which they are total strangers even before their parents set their hands on these, whilst their parents sit happily without sense of revulsion; sometimes the children combine this habit with the emission of foul and unprintable language. When some of these children grow up, because they were never savoir-faire, (lacking the tenets of Aroversity), their outlook in life is one of greed, conquest and perhaps fraudulence. In Arochukwu, I am fortunate to know and have associated with good, well educated (both western-style and Aroversity) men of great wisdom, intelligence, decorum, who have exhibited the best standard of Aro-man worthy of emulation by other Aros and non-Aros. It will be an injustice to those people and a disservice to the present and future generations of Arochukwu if I don't salute these thorough homosapiens and example-personified Aro-men. So to you my friends, I say "well done."

Chapter Three

WESTERN EDUCATION

Apart from Aroversity, there were various ancient institutions mainly of Christina origin, where the Aros received Western style education. I attended one of such schools namely Church of Scotland Mission School at Obinkita Village. Slessor Memorial Home was a convent and day school for girls and Hugh Goldie had, during my childhood, shifting usage. Hugh Goldie was at one time a pastoral college, sometime women teacher training college ("Ndi Mgbe Ncha"); in 1949, Sir Francis Akanu Ibiam (as he then was), a medical practitioner and missionary was running a medical clinic at Hugh Goldie. It has since reverted to its original role as a pastoral college. And, apart from the above establishments, there were at one time a government school at Arochukwu – the present site of Aggrey Primary School.

Aggrey Memorial College had been founded by that great sage, late Dr Alvan Ikoku in 1932 and was the only secondary school from Arochukwu to Umuahia on one flank and from Arochukwu to Calabar on another flank, Port-Harcourt on another flank and Onitsha on the other. There were only the Government College Umudike – Umuahia, Hope Waddell and St. Patrick Colleges in Calabar; Christ the King's College and Dennis Memorial Grammar School Onitsha and Aggrey Memorial College Arochukwu – few institutions existed in those days, many other schools were not approved. There was also another school owned and run by late Mazi T.K Utchey – Jubilee School which gave the road leading to it the name – Jubilee Road. This school was taken over by the Arochukwu people in 1949 and renamed Arochukwu National School, and late educationist Mazi S.O Nwangoro was made its headmaster. However, because of financial constraints due to inability of the Aros to support the school financially particularly in payment of teachers' salaries, the whole scheme of a National School fizzled out. However, when the school was under the headmastership of late Mazi S.O. Nwangoro, the highest standard of education was maintained and the school was second to none. The site can still be seen at the border between Obinkita Village and Amaoba villages along Jubilee Road Arochukwu but few people know today that the name "Jubilee" was attributable to late Mazi T.K. Utchey the designer of the Arochukwu emblem "Omu-Aro."

Early Arochukwu Educated Men

The early Arochukwu educated men were mainly teachers. Prominent among them were late Dr Alvan Ikoku, late Mazi T.K Utchey; late Teacher Moses Onwuchekwa; late Mazi S.O. Nwangoro; late headmaster and one time supervising teacher Emmanuel Oti; Madam Mgbafor Udo; late Nwafor Udo; late Mazi Ogwuma Nwafor; late Barrister Edward Kanu Uku and Madam Mgboro Ekeagba; among the later generation, are late Okoro Dike; Mazi Emmanuel Nnabugwu; Mazi Frank Okereke; Re. Dan Nnabugwu; late Miss Lillie Moses; Miss Aina Uwakwe; Miss Maria James (now Mrs Achinivu); late Miss Peace Oti; Miss Nnenaya Ukoha (Mrs Eni); Mazi Emmanuel Eni; Late Mazi Uwanta Okorafor; Mazi U.U. Udonsi and Dr Julie N. Onwuchekwa (now Professor).

The early graduates known to me apart from late Dr Ikoku were late Barrister Edward Kanu Uku – the first Arochukwu Lawyer who returned to Arochukwu in 1949; Mazi S.G. Ikoku; late Mr. Chima Oji (a one-time principal of McGregor College Afikpo); late Mazi Pius Igboko; Mazi K.C. Okoronkwo; late Mazi K.C. Okoro and Professor Chimere Ikoku. Other Aro graduates were of Aros in diaspora – they could be counted by the fingers.

Sports and Sporting Activities

Although there were various sporting activities which I watched in Arochukwu town e.g. the wrestling contest at Ibom on "Nkwo-Ekpe Ibom Day", during the yam festival, lawn tennis played by my father, the late Headmaster Emmanuel Oti and some white men at the Barracks (Arochukwu Government Station), "koso" and "otikpaa" contests by youths on the sand, football match at Aggrey College (inter-house matches) and among the various schools in Arochukwu, the main annual event was the sporting activities at the British Empire Day celebrations at the playing-field (the present site of the Arochukwu main market.) "Koso" was a conically shaped and tinkered plaything which when spun on the ground, rotates, or dances on the ground (resembles a spinning top). "Otikpaa" was similarly shaped but was made of wood. Some are indeed fanciful. The "otikpaa" was thrashed every now and again when rotating, so that rotation continued.

The British Empire Day was the sports of all sports as every school in the Arochukwu district namely: Aro Mission School, Sang School, Ikpe School, Ututu School, Ihe School, Aggrey Primary School, Obio Usere School, including Aggrey Memorial College attended. There was a march-past by all schools and the white district officer mounted a platform and took the salute. Thereafter, the sporting activities and competition commenced. It was at one such games in 1939 that Miss Julie Onwuchekwa (Professor Julie Onwuchekwa) and late Miss Peace Oti (Mrs Uwakwe) won and were presented with enamel mugs. At a meeting held at the Barracks in 1949 (when the venue changed) headmaster Nkem Ijoma Nkem and one Nwanko Ibekwe excelled in the sprinting event. Mr Otusi Omoji Otusi a student of Aggrey Memorial College was unbeatable in the 1946 games. A girl from Ututu Town by name Miss Atuma Okorie, won most of the women prices in 1949, except the few collected by my younger sister Miss Rose Onwuchekwa (late Mrs Rose Aka). Asang Brass Band was in attendance to add colour and pageantry to the whole activities. Whilst the sellers of all manner of food and soft drinks were at hand to entertain the majority whose main purpose of attendance was the bazaar, rather than the sporting activities.

In the game of football, the following were very prominent players, Mazi Mkpa Nwoke; Mr Abili, Mazi Emmanuel Nnabugwu and at the Aggrey College level were Mazi Erasmus Okoroji who was also a great sprinter and John Onyeador who later on, played regularly for Nigeria and was one of the indefatigable trio of "Onyeanwuna", "Onyeador" and "Onyeali". The three "Onyes" of the late 1950s.

Politics

In the late 1940's, politics was rearing its head in Arochukwu. Those of us who were privileged to read our fathers copies of the "NIGERIAN EASTERN MAIL" said to be published by one Mr. Clinton came across such names as N.C.N.C (National Council of Nigeria and Cameroons), Dr Nnamdi Azikiwe, Mazi Mbonu Ojike, Dr Kingsley Ozumba Mbadiwe, Professor Eyo Ita, Ubani Ukoma, A.C. Nwapa etc. of course Dr Alvan Ikoku was a son of the soil. These names were just names to me and I was too young to appreciate then what politics was all about except that the above names particularly that of Mazi Mbonu Ojike was very impressive because my father was always using the phrase "boycott all boycottables" a phraseology which I now know was invented by the late Mbonu Ojike - an Aro son in diaspora.

Arochukwu was too far from the scene of political activity except that at one time or the other, the late Dr Alvan Ikoku was said to be representing us somewhere and was doing so very well. Being a good friend of my father, my father was always mentioning his name and accomplishments. I only related him to Aggrey Memorial College and particularly the beautiful striped blazer, cap, socks and belt which students of his college proudly wore on the few occasions they were allowed to leave campus. I believe Dr Ikoku's party was called U.N.P. (United National Party) and later U.N.I.P. He was at one time leader of opposition in the Eastern House of Assembly and brought constructive criticism to bear on the proceedings of government. Later, late Senator Udo and late Representative Udenyi were prominent Aro politicians. Politics was still the personal affair of the individuals – organised and financed by the individuals. The Aros did not understand much of politics, the only thing people understood was that "this is our beloved son in whom we are well pleased."

Arochukwu politics took a progressive turn when Mazi S.G. Ikoku returned from overseas. He was down to earth, mixed freely and was outspoken. He was indeed different from the fathers of politics who were there before him and questioned the status quo. I listened to one of his first lectures in early 1950s and that was the first time I heard words like "socialism", "equality", "justice" and "economics". Mazi S.G. Ikoku joined the Action group and although I did not understand the difference between N.C.N.C., the Action group and indeed the other political parties, I must say without any fear of contradiction that it was he, Mazi S.G. Ikoku who brought modern political thought to Arochukwu. He contested and won election to the then Eastern House of Assembly and became Leader of opposition but never believed in money politics.

Healthcare:

In Arochukwu of my childhood, modern healthcare was a nightmare or non-existent. I was lucky to have a knowledgeable father. In the family's medicine chest were all sorts of first-aid medicines, lotions, bandages, iodine, carbolic, quinine (for malaria), castor-oil, aspirin, and others that I cannot remember. He treated us, and everybody else who cared to come around free of charge. For difficult cases, he will send the person to Itu Mission Hospital with a letter. He was well known by the white doctor there. Itu was only a distance of about eighteen miles from Arochukwu, but in those days, it was a day's journey by canoe. The road was atrocious and therefore rarely used.

There was no hospital at Arochukwu. I did not even see a clinic and there was no resident doctor. Dr Akanu Ibiam as then he was, was at Abiriba Mission Hospital a distance of about 45 miles. He only came over to Arochukwu to set up a clinic in 1949 at Hugh Goldie. However, iterant private doctors visited Arochukwu about three times a year on a day's trip. Days before his arrival, the town crier will go around the villages and market places announcing the great event. Every afflicted person looked up to that day like the coming of the Messiah. When the day came, hundreds of people would troop to the venue. Injections were the order of the day. Anyone who did not receive an injection did not believe he had received treatment. If the injection formed an abscess this was evidence that the injection was effective and collecting and killing off all the bad blood and parasites in the body. Antibiotics were in the form of "M&B". These fat tablets were known by their serial numbers. Any ailment which could not be cured was a visitation of God or a curse, of òne juju or one hidden crime or another and was smothered by the forefathers (ndichie) and that was why he could not respond to a cure or medicine.

However, in spite of the non-availability of western style or orthodox medicine, I can proudly say that there were many herbalists and others knowledgeable in the use of herbs, roots and bark of trees or combination of these for the effective treatment of such ailments as malaria, dysentery, hypothermia etc. Many elderly women were good midwives. I was not born in the hospital and likewise my brother and sister before me, but delivered by my maternal and paternal grandmothers both of whom were locally recognised midwives and women came from far and near – brought by their husbands to be delivered in our backyard. The herbalists mentioned above were quite different from native doctors who in those days and today will immerse their cure in mysticism, invocation or exorcism of evil spirits. Unfortunately, most of these herbalists died without passing on their knowledge. Since they were illiterates, no literature of their work was left behind.

Not until the late 1940s and early 1950s when the Arochukwu General Hospital was built that orthodox medicine was administered at our doorstep. These coupled with the reduction of ignorance brought about by education and the joint activities of the then colonial government and the missionaries. For example, sanitary inspectors were employed and these strong-faced individuals in uniform, used to go around every village and compound in Arochukwu to inspect not only the cleanliness of the compound but individual households – particularly the drinking water receptacle or pot ("ite-odido") for mosquitos and their larva. Offenders were fined. This was a good deterrent for environmental uncleanliness and hygiene. The nails and teeth of school children were regularly inspected by their teachers during school drills or morning assembly, before commencement of the day's class-room activities.

Chapter Four

AROCHUKWU TOWN

This beautiful town of environmentally friendly land of God's own people – "Umu-Chukwu" stretches topographically from the Ututu boundary on the Arochukwu – Ohafia road and up and up to a steep-hill through Ugwuakuma Village (the first Arochukwu village from this road) into the heart of Aro-town. On both sides of the hill, before the village of Ugwuakuma, its village people have as long as I can remember, been quarrying and breaking iron-stones for the various building and other construction works in around Arochukwu town. One can still see piles (heaps) of broken iron-stones on both sides of the hill waiting for evacuation. At Ugwuakuma Village is the ancient Arochukwu shrine "the AWADA-ARO." On passing through the "AWADA-ARO" suddenly, the true Aro-man gets an inner feeling of some inexplicable power welcoming him to Arochukwu from a wearisome journey – after all, one would have passed through what is perhaps one of the most atrocious Federal Government-owned roads in Nigeria. Welcome, you are now in the outskirts of the town of Arochukwu – the land of my birth.

The road meandering through a beautiful terrain of evergreen farm and ligneous land of palm and other fruit trees interspersed with residential houses of the Ugwuakuma and the Agbagwu villages, the next, Arochukwu village on this road. From Agbagwu village, a traveller can now see straight before him the Arochukwu Government Station, popularly known as Barracks or "Baraki" as the Arochukwu people call it. It is in fact the government residential area and seat of government.

Barracks: "Baraki"

The Barracks or Baraki as the name implies was the seat of British colonial government in Arochukwu from where administration was carried on after the Arochukwu Conquests of 1901 – 1902. Arochukwu Conquest is said to be the most difficult British colonial engagement in the colonization of Nigeria.

The Barracks sited on a hill overlooking the main town of Arochukwu and what is now part of Cross-River and Akwa-Ibom States is the most beautiful spot in Arochukwu topographically. One can see clearly on any day, the Cross River glittering in the sun, together with the vast land of the Cross-River valley and the town of Itu which is about eighteen miles away in what is now the Akwa-Ibom State. Sometimes, on a clear day, one can see what is said to be parts of the town of Calabar about one hundred miles away and, over it the Cameroun Mountains, rising in the horizon.

Baraki as was pointed out earlier was the seat of colonial administration in Arochukwu. One can still see today, the colonial wooden and corrugated iron-roofed elevated bungalow which was the residence of the then white district officers. I remember vividly well when, these white blokes were carried along by groups of hefty labourers (not of Arochukwu origin) on hammocks, dressed up in safari-suits of khaki and wearing a helmet on their heads. In fact I cannot forget the early impression which I had formed when I saw one or more of these administrators eating banana whilst reclining on the hammock. I had wrongly thought that these strange people ate nothing else but bananas and not until later years did I appreciate that the opposite was the case.

In the D.O's entourage were half clothed or poorly clad labourers carrying loads and were accompanied by one or two stern looking policemen in black clothing, wearing puttees also of black colour (puttees – a long strip of cloth wound spirally round the leg from ankle to knee for protection and support). These policemen carried rifles. As a young man, I was neither afraid of the white D.O. nor the stern looking policemen since I had seen a white missionary and his wife Mr and Mrs Beatie who lived in an elevated wooden and corrugated iron bungalow next to our house at the Obinkita Mission School. And, I had an uncle, the late Mazi Samson Okoronkwo Onwuchekwa in the police force; also in 1946, another uncle of mine late Sergeant Michael Kanu Onwuchekwa was the officer in charge of the Arochukwu police contingent.

Baraki as seat of government had apart from the ancient D.O's elevated wooden bungalow, some other buildings worthy of note. The old postal agency, a concrete and corrugated iron hut, still stands today between the Arochukwu General Hospital and the police station. One Okoro Okorafor from Oror Village was the postal agent. Construction of the present Arochukwu Post Office started about 1946, and construction work of the General Hospital started around the same period – about 1947. Arochukwu has always had a prison although few Arochukwu citizens ever were its inmates. Arochukwu had several well defined procedures and punishments for crimes and criminals which were quicker and were effective deterrent for non-conformity. However, interference of the white D.O. and the white man's court were constant source of friction between the Aro-chiefs and the white D.O. Arochukwu prison, I am told, is one of the oldest prisons in Igbo-land. The old red-brick walled court house is now the magistrate court. The large open grounds of Baraki was well kept during the colonial days and looked much like a first class golf-course although no golf was ever seen by me, played thereat. The only game I saw played was lawn-tennis near the old Rest House at the Agbagwu Village boundary.

Aggrey Memorial College

From the hills of Baraki (barracks), three roads descend into the valley in different directions to what may be properly called Arochukwu-down-town. But, for the old and modern corrugated iron roofs of storey houses that are visible among the wooded terrain of iroko and wild cotton and fruit trees, a first time visitor will not know that beneath this healthy foliage lies the ancient African town of Arochukwu – the land of God's own people (Umu-Chukwu) – a town with a chequered history.

One road leads towards Slessor Memorial Home (as it was then called) and at the junction popularly known as "Nkwu-nabu" "T" junction – named after two beautiful palm-trees) which were somewhere near the location. An arm of the road leads to the famous Aggrey Memorial College – a brain child of that indefatigable late sage and statesman Dr Alvan Ikoku. This college had at one time as some of its pupils such distinguished Nigerians like Mazi Mbonu Ojike (the Boycott King), late Dr Kingsley Ozumba Mbadiwe (K.O Mbadiwe – the man of timber and calibre and a political juggernaut), (now late) Professor U.U. Umozurike and a host of others, I remember reading and memorising the college motto which was conspicuously written on a wall of Abna-Hall, which is the college hall "The soul of all improvements is the improvement of the soul."

Slessor

From Nkwu-nabu "T" junction, one road passes the front of Slessor Memorial Home, which was named after an early Scottish lady missionary – Miss Mary Slessor who was a pioneer in women education in and around Arochukwu town, the town of Calabar and parts of what is now Cross River and Akwa Ibom States. Slessor School was the seat of women education in and around Arochukwu. I do not know the exact date of its establishment but suffice it to say that it is part of

Arochukwu ancient and modern-history. My mother was one of its early students.

At the period covered by my writing, in particular between 1934 and the Second World War, the institution was under the able superintendence of Miss Agnes Arnott (mma-Ezinne) and another short Scottish woman fondly called "daddy" or "mma-mkpumkpu" for her manly behaviour. She was also shorter than Miss Arnott and "mma-mkpumkpu" means "short madam". I knew this woman very well as she was a friend of the family and I was told that it was Ezinne (Mrs Arnott) and herself who brought my parents together. They also baked the wedding cake for their wedding in 1927. Slessor had metamorphosed at various times from a convent, elementary school with women occupational and domestic science centre, into teacher training college and today it is a secondary technical college. The old partly wooden and partly zinc or corrugated iron sheet walled storey building, which was the residence of the above missionaries and later had a Miss Green in occupation has been preserved. However, the present users know neither the history nor the reverence which the Arochukwu mothers and indeed town-folks of yesteryears owe this building, which may be regarded as a symbol of Arochukwu history and a bridge between the old and new culture – culture of women education.

Amanagwu Square

Descending the Slessor hill of clay which was in those days very slippery during the rainy season "Ugwu-Okuko-Uro" (hill of clay), one passes a stream, "the Iyi-ukwu Amanagwu" and then ascends a hillock into Amanagwu Square. But before I tell you more about Amanagwu Square, I want you to share with me some forgotten factor about "Iyi-Ukwu Stream." The stream rises somewhere near the Utugugwu village of Arochukwu Town, a village predominantly of Okennachi kindred where it is joined by another stream near the moderate waterfall at "Osu-gworo-gworo" and then meanders through what was then a thick forest (but now inhabited by people) and is called "Iyi-Ukwu Obinkita" in the area where it crosses the road at Obinkita Village land, where it is the main source of drinking water.

The Iyi-Ukwu Obinkita stream was so sacred that fishing and splashing was forbidden. In those days a colony of large fresh-water voracious barracuda-like fish were frequently seen swimming at the upper serene part of the stream. They were supposed to be of the gods and sacrifices were frequently offered at an "Achi-tree" at the bank of the stream. The stream was deified since it was perennial as against other streams like "Nwesen" and "Ngele" which dried-up in the dry season.

The stream also at Obinkita section was said by oral tradition to be a stream of justice during the slave traded era and any runaway slave who was pursued by his master regained his freedom once he jumped into the stream. He is said to have taken refuge with the gods and, if his master in anger throws a spear or shoots an arrow at him or jumps into the stream to beat him up, such master would have desecrated the holy stream by unworthy pollution for which a substantial fine was imposed which will include presentation of a cow or other domestic animals to the community for sacrifice to appease the gods of the stream. Sometimes, he was required to donate several slaves to the chiefs of Arochukwu because the pollution was also said to affect not only the stream at Obinkita but had continued to offend the down-stream at Ibom and Amanagwu villages which also are sources of portable water.

Obinkita is predominantly of Ezeagwu kindred and likewise Amanagwu village. Ibom village is of the Ibom-isii kindred. Iyi-ukwu stream passes through the three Arochukwu kindreds of Okennachi, Ibom-isii and Ezeagwu, and was importantly historically.

Mgbala-Ekpe Amanagwu

I now come back to Amanagwu square. At the Amanagwu square was the most beautiful "Mgbala-Ekpe" – Ekpe Fraternity House in the 1940s and 1950s. Ekpe was the executive and sometimes judicial arm of Arochukwu ancient government. Each village has its own "Mgbala-Ekpe." Each Ekpe fraternity can only enforce discipline within its own jurisdictional village. If enforcement is required outside a person's village, it is only "Ekpe-Aro" – Arochukwu Central Ekpe which has that jurisdiction. The Mgbala-Ekpe Amanagwu was of red mud walls with thatched roof. On the walls of which were painted the most beautiful ancient Arochukwu designs, symbols and pictures. Some of the symbols (Nsibiri) communicated messages of represented events which occurred a long time ago. There were also paintings of wild animals that were said to have inhabited parts of Arochukwu such as leopards, elephants, buffalos, etc. I understand that the paintings were the designs and handiwork of that indefatigable unassuming artists, sculptor and wood carver, Mazi Oti-Nwa-Oti of Ibom Village. It is sad to note that this great "Mgbala-Ekpe" a great symbol of our past, had to make room for the widening of the road during its macadamization but its memory will ever linger on in my mind.

I heard of Mazi Oti-Nwa-oti for a very long time before I grew up to make his acquaintance. It was in 1946 when he was commissioned by my late father to engrave or write his initials on all his household furniture and expensive utensils. Whenever I look at some of these objects bearing this sage's engraving or writing, they remind me of a forgotten master artist – a Michael-Angelo, a Rembrandt or Ben Enwonwu of Arochukwu Kingdom. In 1974, he had specially made for me, as a token of our friendship an Arochukwu-style chalk-trough (Arianzu). I am sure many of his works of art adorn many other family homes in Arochukwu.

Ujari Village

Turning left off the main artery road, through part of Amanagwu village, one comes to a Presbyterian Church (formerly Church of Scotland Mission Amanagwu). The present church, replaces the old church which I knew, which stood at the same spot. Immediately after the church is the historical market of NCHEGE or NCHEGE-IBOM. This was the largest market in and around Arochukwu during the colonial days. It convened every four days (not a daily market) and as such attracted traders and customers from neighbouring Igbo, Efik and Ibibio towns (now part of the Cross-River and Akwa-Ibom states.)

The market convened and the people converged on the Nkwo-market day, which is one of the Igbo market days of Nkwo, Eke, Orie and Afor (Avor). During the annual Ikeji Yam Festival, on Nkwo-Nzukoro or Nkwo-eresi (eresi is rice) as that Nkwo market day was called, the market was so full and overflowing with people, foodstuff, yams, domestic animals for sale and assortments of imported goods, (particularly textiles of Indian Madras cloth (George) and other types. Human go-slow was created everywhere, that it was virtually impossible to locate a wanted friend, customer or relative. This gave rise to an Arochukwu idiom that "Nchege – Ibom avugi nde guzoro-oto ya buru nde choro ino-onodi." That is to say that the Nchege market does not accommodate all people who wanted merely to stand up or pass by how much more of the people who wanted to sit on chairs. In other words, a demand, a request or expectation was frivolous in the circumstance.

Opposite the Nchege Market, is the storey building of late Mazi Ekubo of Ujari Village. This building has stood the test of time and it was at one time the most beautiful residential storey house in this vicinity. It is still well maintained by his children. After the Ekubo House, you are now at Ujari Square with a famous "Obu" seating place for the elders in the afternoon. It serves also as a place of informal discussions, surveillance of intruders and strangers alike and acts as a sort of fortification.

Ulonta Ndi – Okoroji

The most famous Arochukwu Ulonta (family house) is the Ulonta Ndi-Okoroji at Ujari Village. It is also the most famous such ancient family house in Igbo Nation. It is a house of history of Arochukwu and Igbo Nation. Built as a sort of amphitheatre and equipped centuries ago, it has been classified as a national museum by the National Commission for Museums and Monuments. I understand that its maintenance is now subvented by the Federal Government. A visit to Arochukwu is incomplete without a visit to this ancient museum. However, its doors are not open to persons whether of Arochukwu or elsewhere who have certain disabilities – violators always incur the wrath of the Arochukwu gods and of the spirit of dead forbears (Ndichie). Visitors are politely interrogated before admission.

At the back of Ujari Village is Amasu Village – an ancient river port and a fishing port of great potentiality. The port would have played a prominent role during the slave trade era as a port of embarkation for that obnoxious cargo, through the Enyong Creek and Cross-River to the port of Calabar for evacuation to the Americas.

Ibom Village

Immediately from Amanagwu village on the Baraki – Slessor – Amanagwu – Ibom main road is Ibom Village. Ibom Village is also accessible from the Arochukwu Government Station (Baraki) directly through the "Iyi-Ukwu-Ibom" Stream. Before the construction of the Arochukwu General Hospital which blocked part of the road, the Baraki-Ibom road was the main artery road from Baraki to Ibom and to Arochukwu heart-land.

Ibom Village of my childhood was so significant in my memory as the place where modern concrete or stone residential storey houses first sprang up in Arochukwu.

Although I am older than any of these buildings yet they are now over fifty years of age and deserve to be separated from their more modern counterparts. The houses stood and still stand like colossus not far from each other and some of them have names inscribed or written prominently on them for example, "Opobo House", "Hope Villa" and so on.

Ibom Village of my childhood was also significant in that it at one time had a government school which was administered by the then British colonial government of Nigeria. When the government pulled out, the site was taken over and renamed Aggrey primary School to save the site from total abandonment.

Aburuma – Ibom

And in spite of the modern houses and of the presence of the government school or Aggrey Primary School, Ibom Village was also the home of the fearsome shrine of the women cult "ABURUMA" or "ABARAMA" which functioned beneath a wooded grove of iroko and wild-cotton trees which in effect concealed whatever rituals that were performed there. It was a taboo for any man to cast his eyes on the cult members during their not often nocturnal performance out of their shrine. Their monotone drumming, shrieky and screechy songs would send signals loud and clear to all intruders to beware or face the grave consequences.

I remember very well on one occasion about 1942, we were returning from Itu town by river canoe. Itu Town, only a distance of about eighteen miles through a very atrocious road, which was partly flooded during the rainy season, and equally impassable during the dry season on account of the numerous broken low wooden bridges or wooden planks carelessly placed over the rivers, streams and part of the creek.

River canoe was therefore the only alternative to road transport for people wishing to get to the town of Itu and from Itu either to Ikot-Ekpene town or Aba by road or to Calabar by larger river canoe which looked more like a gondola. The voyage from Itu town takes all day and sometimes, runs into the night. Most passengers will disembark at "Onuasu Nwabeke" (government beach) which was itself several miles to my village at Arochukwu.

On this fateful day, we arrived the government beach at night and by the time we had trekked with our belongings passing through the Aggrey Memorial College, Slessor, Amanagwu Village, and then to Ibom Village on our way to our own village, it was fast approaching midnight. To our greatest agony and helplessness, this all female mystery cult members had temporarily imposed a curfew and all movement of passers-by in the area became immediately restricted. The hair on my body rose as I was under an extreme fear on hearing their shrieky and screechy unmelodious songs. We were quickly advised by an old man who was plodding towards us in the dark, who was almost noiseless except for the sound made by his walking stick, to return to Amanagwu Village and stay there till day light returned. And, we did as advised. When we eventually passed through, the whole square was dead silent as the sweet sound of silence had returned.

Ibom Village square was also prominent as the traditional venue in Arochukwu where wrestling contest takes place during the annual New Yam Festival (Ikeji). On the last Nkwo-market day immediately preceding the "Eke-Ekpe" day, Arochukwu youths will assemble in this square to challenge one another to wrestling contest as evidence of manhood or coming of age. This a significant part of Arochukwu culture. I must state that I was not privileged during my youth to have wrestled in this square, either because I was not allowed or because at the time there were equally other challenges and avenues to prove oneself.

Eze Aro's Palace

Descending the hillock from Ibom Village and passing through "Nwesen Ibom" Stream which dried up or was cut-off in pockets during the dry season, but turning into a great river during the rain, one passes through the ancient palace of the paramount ruler of Arochukwu – the Eze Aro of Arochukwu (Arochukwu Monarch) and the Oror Village, where it situates and with the "Ukwu – Ovor Shrine." Oror occupies a dual position as a palace and as a village. Near the entrance to the palace compound is the old Arochukwu council house.

Africa Road

The Africa Road links the Eze-Aro's palace and the Amaikpe Square in Obinkita Village. The road was so named after an old church building (The Africa Church) situate along this very broad road. The Obinkita Village people also call this road "Uzo Okwara Odo". It was and is still one of the most important stretches of roads in Arochukwu, as it is the Arochukwu Apian-way. In times of celebration such as Ikeji Festival or Christmas, anyone who had not passed through this stretch of toad, would not have a great feeling of the celebration. It suddenly turns into a parade ground for beautiful girls and handsome young men. And, in spite of the intense heat, sometimes attendant to the period of most Arochukwu celebrations, it is comforting to watch people walking to and fro this road happily in the mood of the celebration appropriately attired for each occasion.

Amaikpe Square: Obinkita Village

Amaikpe Square which is at the Obinkita Village, as the name implies, means a court or judgment square. "Ama" means a square and "Ikpe" means trial (a court). It is the widest of Arochukwu ancient squares and has multipurpose uses. It was a place for the public trial of offenders for the most invidious crimes such as murder, treachery against Arochukwu Nation, disruption of Arochukwu in its legitimate trade, levying war against Arochukwu town or one of its colonies or settlements, divulging Arochukwu Nation secrets to strangers or unbelievers. For example, as to the Arochukwu Long-Juju (Ibinukpabi) etc.

The above offences being heinous crimes were required to be tried in public on the principle that "justice must not only be done but must be seen to be done." However, an accused person had little chance of acquittal since his accusers were also the judges. Trial was by ordeal. The first prisoners said to be tried in his ancient square were some of the captives of inter-tribal warfare, during the war for the establishment of Arochukwu Kingdom. Subsequently other trials followed of town-folks, whose crimes were regarded as reprehensible as that of those who waged war on Arochukwu or had resisted Arochukwu domination. Amaikpe is also the place where Osim was said to have lost blood. Stones of Union or Unity Square, marks the very spot.

Ikeji Festival

The Annual Ikeji Yam festival was said at first by oral tradition not to be a yam festival at all but rather, the celebration of the anniversary of the victory of the Aro-war. The victory in that war and the subsequent trial at Amaikpe Square of the leaders of the rebels who levied war against Arochukwu brought a great joy to many. It was a great occasion with dancing, drinking, and merry making. And the braves of war (soldiers) were rewarded with beautiful brides. The beginning of "Mgbede culture" i.e., (fattening of girls for marriage). Several domestic animals were slaughtered and yams and other edible tubers were brought in by the neighbouring Igbo towns of Ututu and Ihechiowa and these combined very well with the spirit of the occasion. However, as time went on, when the relationship between Aros and their previous enemies had been normalized, the celebration ceased to be a celebration of war victory and was instead known as the Ikeji New yam Festival. It is not intended in this work to narrate the events of the Ikeji New Yam Festival.

The Aros are traditionally not great farmers, but merchants, diplomats and administrators. Oral tradition had it that during one such Ikeji New Yam festival, there were virtually no yams available in Arochukwu markets and, the people and the Aro monarch, were incensed by the affront of their immediate farming neighbours which they considered as treachery. The chiefs of these towns were quickly summoned before the Arochukwu monarch to explain their action. Their defence was that the yams in the particular season were immature and puny – that they did not want to insult the great Arochukwu people by selling to them immature yams for a great celebration. Samples of the puny yams were presented as evidence and reparations were made to avoid the anger of Ibinukpabi. Ever since this diplomatic incident or 'yam palaver' the Ututu people were expected to savour the new yams first before the celebration of Ikeji Arochukwu. This has led to a rhyme sang by Arochukwu children as follows:

"Ututu rie ji Aro e-rie, Aro buru-uzo echere, ahaa"

In 1947, when I was living with one of my late uncles, an Aroman and a school teacher at Amaodu Ututu, a very old Ututu man – a friend of my late uncle (because my uncle from time to time brings him a container of tobacco ground by my maternal grandmother at Arochukwu) said during one of their conversations, that his father had informed him that it was an Arochukwu trader on a handsome payment, who fashioned out Ututu's defence, and thereby averted the invocation of a serious reprisal from the Aros. To which my late uncle exclaimed in bewilderment "Aro!" shaking his head. I pretended not to have listened. So you can see that it takes an Aro man and not an outsider, to undo an Aro man.

On the last "Affor" (Avor) market day called "avor-osu" during the Ikeji Festival, there was a great display of dancing by the "ekpo" masquerades mounted by the inhabitants of the plantations of Obinkita Village. The display and prowess of the masquerades were outstanding and electrifying. Usually, many Aro people will assemble at Amaikpe Square Obinkita, to watch the display. No other village in Arochukwu was traditionally allowed to mount a similar display on that particular day.

Women, particularly young women, watched from the side-line and distance and stampeded or ran away, when a masquerade approached so as to avoid being injured or maimed by a masquerade, as this incident was common in those days. Young men, except the initiated, were equally not spared; thrashing or scorching by a particular masqueraded called "Nkita-Oku" which carried flaming fire and sword (akangkang) were common occurrence. After all, "Ekpo" masquerades are supposed to be spirits and the uninitiated are not supposed to see spirits. I enjoyed watching the masquerades and as most Obinkita sons were fully initiated, I had no fear except in the hands of a rascally performer. The drumming energised every Obinkita youth and elder and most people could dance to the drums. To most Aro youths, this is the Ikeji Festival – the Eke-Ekpe being the climax of the celebration.

Chapter Five

Eke-Ekpe Day

Eke-Ekpe day is the climax of the Ikeji Yam Festival. On this last "Eke Market day", most Aro men, women and children will assemble at the Amaikpe Square at Obinkita Village to celebrate the yam festival, and each of the nineteen Arochukwu villages are expected to and do bring one or more dancing or masquerade troupes to perform at the square. The festival brings together once a year many Aro sons and daughters at home, from the settlements and in diaspora and serves as the main channel whereby ancestral links are maintained for generations. The Ikeji celebrations also serve as a family link of the Aros through their maternal ancestry "Ikwu" or caste system.

When I was growing up, I heard much talk of "Ikwu" the names that were variously spoken of are "Azuma-Eze", "Ndi-Eni", "Ikwu-Oko", "Ibe-Ngwere", "Ibe-Avia", "Ikwu-Obo", "Ikwu-Mmaku", "Ibe-Aka" and "Ibe-Oriewu". I did not know what these names or caste systems stood for except that I was said to belong to one of them. And, during the Ikeji festivals, some older visitors who had come from far away villages in Arochukwu were quick to remind me that I was their kith and kin and a member of their "Ikwu" (caste). Some of them – particularly the older women would hug me dearly in their arms. My father will give some of these people some money for their celebration of Ikeji as they were about to leave – that is after they had been lavishly entertained.

Ikeji festival was celebrated by all Arochukwu people – non-Christians and Christians alike but Christians did not indulge in the fetish aspects of the celebration such as cooking and offering the "Osu" and animals' blood, kolanut, and white chalk (nzu) to the idols and shrines. My father, being a school teacher and elder in the Church respected the tradition but, he like other missionaries of his days, never indulged in the fetishness of the celebration. Ikeji celebration was nevertheless in our house a joyous period and visitors were entertained just like during the Christmas celebrations. We all were allowed to go to the Amaikpe Square to watch the celebrations properly attired as was befitting in Arochukwu tradition. My mother will lend me Indian Madras Cloth (George cloth) which was tied on my loin by a bigger relative and I would wear on top a white shirt, either my own (when I was older), or another borrowed garment from my father or older relation.

Girls also tied Indian-madras cloth and with appropriate blouses. (Girls from illiterate parentage wore a group of beads – usually red or black on their loins with delicate body designs painted on their body ("uri" or "nkasi-ala"). Adult females of the family wore Indian-madras (George cloth), with appropriate blouses and head-ties and held umbrellas and white handkerchiefs. The male elders were attired in befitting jumpers (isi-inyinya) and similarly tied Indian-madras cloth and wore either a panama hat or a woollen knitted overlapping hat and carried a walking stick when attending the celebrations at Amaikpe Square. Non-Aros were known immediately on sight, by their clumsy attire of trousers and short knickers or gowns.

In fact, I observed when I was young, that when an Aro-man is properly attired with his walking stick and walking to the Amaikpe Square to attend a celebration, which was the most important event on that day for him, (which engages his full attention,) if he was in passing asked of the name of the capital of Nigeria for example, his quick response will be "Amaikpe"; not because he does not know the answer but because his attention is concentrated only on the one thing of importance to him in the world and that is Amaikpe Square and the celebration going on there. The only other matter equally of importance to him on that blessed day is security. Aroman is always security conscious and even on Eke-Ekpe day not every person troops to Amaikpe. Some able-bodied men are deliberately allowed to stay behind by villages and families as strategy against surprise attack by enemies and thieves who may want to exploit the situation for their nefarious activities. So was the importance of Eke-Ekpe day to the Aro people.

Since the end of the Nigerian civil war, I had attended several Ikeji celebrations and Eke-Ekpe day at Amaikpe Square. On few occasions, I have been appalled by the range, style and type of dressing by fellow Aro-men and women particularly the "nouveau-riche" who wear anything from babariga, agbada, to English type suits on Eke-Ekpe day. And rather than hide behind the crowd as being improperly clad, try to make themselves conspicuous. The celebrations marking the official burial of the late Arochukwu monarch (Eze Aro) Mazi Kanu Oji in 1987 saw the Aro people put their best feet forward in the style, type and dignity reminiscent of Aro people and for which they are known throughout Igboland and the former eastern Nigeria. The "Omu-Aro" specially designed Indian Madras Cloth was not invented at the time covering the early period of my writing, although, the "Omu" emblem had been in existence. Since its introduction, as the official cloth of the Aro-people, those who could not afford to acquire an Omu-cloth, are still permitted by tradition to tie a plain Indian-madras cloth. "Ukara" loin-cloth is however used by men who had been fully initiated in the traditional "Ekpe-na-Mboko" society.

Amaikpe Square: As a Market

Amaikpe Square was a daily market – in fact the only daily market in Arochukwu. "Nchege Market" as was stated earlier, convened once in every four days on "Nkwo" market day. Amaikpe convened daily even on "Nkwo" market day although "Nchege" would attract more buyers and sellers on that day. Most shoppers will visit both markets on the same day in search of particular bargains. On the "Avor" – Osu" market day, during the Ikeji Yam Festival, Amaikpe was so full and extended beyond its bounds. Every item of foodstuff and agricultural product known to the Igbo man were seen in the market. In spite of the occasional stampede, the Obinkita elders saw to it that the traders were not so molested.

In the year 1949, the white District Officer thought that Arochukwu Town was ripe for the creation of a super daily market similar to that at Aba, Ikot-Ekpene, Calabar, Itu and Umuahia. Without consultation or little consultation with all the elders of Arochukwu, he tried to impose "Nchege market" on the Aros as the daily market. This in effect would have meant the closure of all other markets (Amaikpe and Ekuku). The attempted imposition was resisted by the Amuze people comprising thirteen Arochukwu villages out of the nineteen villages, made up of Oror; Utugugwu; Obinkita; Amakwu; Isimkpu; Amanagwu; Atani; Amukwa; Amaoba; Ugbo; Ugwuavo; Asaga, and Amuvi. I remember attending one or two of their protest meetings at the D.O's residence with my father led by the late Eze Kanu Oji (the Eze Aro) with late Mazi Ogbonaya Anicho (Eze Ogo Obinkita) and the representatives of other villages in the group. I was not part of the delegation as I was a small fry but merely carried along my father's documents as he was their spokesman and interpreter. After a long relentless struggle, Amaikpe and Ekuku (Eke-Ukwu) were repreived and Amaikpe was instead widened to its present perimeter by clearing of the old "Achi-trees" which clustered at the square and almost obstructed Amankwu Village from view, when standing near the great Iroko tree (oji-ogo).

Various backyards of families bordering the square were with the consent of their owners handed over to the Amuze community which was now rechristened "Amaeze" by my father – the late Teacher Moses .A. Onwuchekwa, because to him the word "Amuze" was derogatory and connotes "jungle" or primitive (since the Eze Aro lives in one of the villages (Oror) comprised in the area). The proper name he argued should be "Amaeze" – this was unanimously adopted. Today, there is Amaeze Parish, Amaeze Union, etc. My father was so much in love with his new coinage or invented name that he subsequently christened my son "Amaeze".

At the junction of Africa Road and Jubilee Road, immediately before Amaikpe square, is the famous Obinkita Hall, built near the site of the old public toilets. Construction work started about 1949 but actual commissioning was in early 1950s. It stands as a symbol of community effort.

Amaoba Village & Ngeleokwo

At the end of the Africa Road, just before it joined the Amaikpe Square, is Jubilee Road, named after a school of the same name along the road, a creation of late educationist T.K Utchey of Ujari Village. The school at one time (about 1949) changed to Arochukwu National School. Today, it has another name and is under different management. Jubilee Road runs into Amaoba Village – another ancient river port used for transportation to Itu Town and the town of Calabar. This river is called "Ngeleokwo". I loved swimming about in the river and had been transported there by passenger canoe from Itu Town, as it is quite near to my village and was a better alternative to stopping at the Government Beach (Onuasu Nwa Beke). When road transportation improved into the Igbo heartland, commerce and transportation through Ngeleokwo no longer presented a viable option. Today, it wears the look of abandonment and neglect although still serving the riparian rice farmers as inland water system, for the transportation of rice and other agricultural products.

Arochukwu Mission School and Church

At the southern end of Obinkita is the Arochukwu Mission School and Church established by the Church of Scotland Mission. It is an ancient institution. Most Arochukwu educated men and women of old, attended this ancient primary school. My father was one of its pupils before 1920 and most of my brothers and sisters including myself had our early education in this school. We also resided in the mission premises when my father was a teacher there. At that time the school was run by the Church of Scotland Mission and was the dominant primary school in the area covered by the old Arochukwu district, Abiriba, Ohafia and Bende Division. A white man and his wife, rev Beatie (Beatty) lived there in an elevated wooden and corrugated iron bungalow which is still preserved together with the ancient corrugated iron walled hut which was the bookshop. I collected my first school writing slate and slate pencil from my father in this bookshop. He was a teacher at the school and incidentally also in charge of the bookshop. He handed over to late Mazi Moses Odinkemere in 1942 when he was promoted and transferred to Asaga Ohafia Mission School as its headmaster.

There was little distinction between church and school as the two were under the same management. The teachers were also missionaries and some of them were also elders of the church. There was an old church building where children of my age once attended Sunday school classes. I have a vague recollection of church services being conducted in the old church, before the move to the present church building. I do not know when construction of the present church building commenced. It must have been commenced before my birth but living in the mission premises with my parents and late headmaster (later supervising teacher) Emmanuel Oti and of course Rev. and Mrs Beatie, I have an early childhood reminiscence of the news that a white carpenter, one Mr Bruckett accidentally fell from the roof of the church building into a drum and fractured his arm and was taken back to England for treatment.

The church elders of the time were mainly septuagenarians or octogenarians who had grey hairs. They were knowledgeable and most of them were very influential leaders of thought in their communities. I can recall a few names – Elder Ujwu Okoro, Elder Okoroafor Udo, Elder Adiele (Anyaele) and Elder Nwonye (or Ivuonye). The new church has very beautiful stained glass. Whenever I attend this church, for whatever purpose, I cannot remove my eyes from these stained glasses as the inscription and portraits bring back past memories. Some of its past pastors who were well known to me were Rev. Beatie; Rev. Olugu from Ebem Ohafia; Very Rev Alfred Anicho from Amuvi Village and later late Reverend P.B. Onwuchekwa. Although I knew other Arochukwu pastors like late Rev. Uwakwenta and late Rev. Mmadunta but I do not know now whether it was in connection with this church.

Eke-Ukwu Market:

Outside the fences of the Church of Scotland Mission and School and separated by the main road, was the Eke-Ukwu market pronounced "Ekuku" in Isimkpu Village. It, like the Nchege market, convened every four days but on "Eke Market day". During the Ikeji New Yam festival, on the "Eke-Odu" market day, it was filled to the brim, spilling over and almost joining Amaikpe. All neighbouring Igbo, Akwa Ibom and Cross-River towns will bring their farm products for display and sale. In those days, there were a lot of foodstuffs in Arochukwu.

Ekuku Market convened under a group of Achi trees with protruding large roots which formed buttresses and extended their limbs in various directions. On these buttresses, some traders could be seen sitting to sell their products. Sometimes, young children stumbled against these protrusions.

This area of Isimkpu Village is now adorned by modern residential houses as the Achi trees and their buttresses, together with this ancient market have given way to social development. Amaikpe daily market now convenes as evening food market at a little corner of the square whilst at every other corner of the square are supermarkets, stores, restaurants, chemist stores and even a bank. Nchege market is only a bare skeleton of its glorious past. The demise of these ancient markets has created room for a modern daily market at the site of the former playing-field along the Obinkita Baraki Road.

Opposite the junction of Atani Village, at Isimkpu is a very old iron fabricated storey house said to have belonged to late Chief Okoro Ume of Isimkpu Village. This building is very interesting as the only house in Arochukwu which I saw during my childhood and even today which has complete steel structure. The owner died without its completion and although completely roofed at the time, the steel structure stood like a giant among others as a symbol of ancient wealth of the Aros. The building had since been completed by the children of the original owner and perhaps not quite to the specification conceptualised by the original owner.

Atani Village and other Villages

Apart from Atani Village which was so prominent in my early mind because it was the Atani Village people who first built a modern village hall at Arochukwu to be followed later by Obinkita village hall, I knew of the existence and had in fact on few occasions in the company of my father, visited the villages of Amangwu (the village of his maternal ancestors): Asaga; Amukwa; Ugbo; Amuvi and Ugwuavor but I did not at the period associate much with these villages as means of transportation was non-existent in those days. Amuvi Village was a great and tiresome trek from my village and foot-travel was the only means of local transportation at the time. However, I knew some of the prominent leaders of these villages either through attendance at the church or during their visits to my father. Some of those of my generation were at the mission school with me although in various classes.

Amuvi Village was also significant to me because of one "Giant Alakuku" (Nwokoro) who was said to be an Amuvi-man. Although I had heard much of him, I did not see him until early 1950 both at Umuahia and Aba since he was not residing at Arochukwu Town. I was taken to see him by an uncle and people paid money to see him. This colossus was said to be more than eight feet tall and was very huge. He had a sore on his big toe where, it was alleged that his main nerve was dismembered to immobilise him as his powers also were said to be beyond human like the legendary giants of Greek mythology. It is said that the colossus has since died.

Chapter Six

AROCHUKWU ANCIENT STOREY HOUSES

Arochukwu was blessed with early wealth and this was evidenced by the existence of ancient storey houses owned by Arochukwu sons of the time, to usher in early western civilisation into the town. Many of such houses were seen by me in some Arochukwu villages notably at Obinkita; Ibom Village (late Elder Adiele's house). There was one such building at Amangwu Village but, apart from those at Obinkita Village, and maybe one or two others, all the rest had collapsed for want of repairs and maintenance. Still standing like three sisters and well maintained to their original standards at the Ndi-agor Compound of Obinkita Village are three ancient storey houses owned by late Mazi Obasi Onwuchekwa, late Moses .A. Onwuchekwa and late Mazi Job Okoro respectively. These buildings standing in close proximity to one another are some of the surviving remnants of an era, to remind us of our social and economic heritage. Families to whom these buildings belong are always willing to show responsible visitors around.

The Tunnel Bridge and Legend of Botched Railway Line

The third axial road from Baraki passes through Hugh Goldie Mission establishment and over the Tunnel Bridge through the playing fields (site of the present Arochukwu Modern Market), through parts of Obinkita Village farm lands, through Ugwuavor Village farm lands and heading to unknown destination. Legend had it that the British Colonial Government had intended a railway line to traverse this very wide track of road linking Port Harcourt through Aba Town on one end and Umuahia – Ibeku on the other through Bende Town. It was understood that the Aros feared that the passing of trains to and fro their land would bring undesirable persons into the town. And, more importantly, that the womenfolk will be induced to run away from home to the bright lights of the cities (male chauvinism and domination). And, as a result of mounting pressure, the project was said to be abandoned.

Whether or not this legend is true or false, one thing is certain that whoever conceived the idea of this bridge across a ravine and filled the top to its present height for a road to be constructed over, had a purpose for this bridge – of course that purpose may never be known. I had on several occasions waded through the fast running water under the bridge from end to end with my peer group during firewood fetching expeditions. It is a massive concrete tunnel over a swift flowing rocky stream. And it is Iyi-ukwu Obinkita flowing eastwards to the Iyiukwu Ibom etc. At the top of the bridge, standing on the main road, the stream produces a deep noise because of contact with the rocks and its speed and is therefore called "Osu dim dim" at this spot because of the noise.

CONCLUSION

I have taken you on a round trip of Arochukwu of my childhood, which is quite different from Arochukwu today with its state of the art dream houses depicting the life style of the modern rich and famous. Arochukwu of my childhood was rich in culture, and there was dignity of speech and dignity of person. As was stated in the preface, the intention of this book is merely to share my childhood reminiscence with the reader and also encourage knowledgeable Aro citizens to write on some aspects of our history, rich culture and social heritage and to leave something for posterity. There is a wealth of interesting aspects of an Aro-man and his God-given kingdom. I have merely mentioned some aspects without discussion, leaving discussion to students, scholars and researchers of these God's own people, to wake-up from their slumber and put their wealth of knowledge on paper – for only by doing so can our culture and rich social heritage be preserved.

In a work like this written through the tender eyes of childhood, there are bound to be errors of time and of events for I am only human and to err is human. Such errors (if they occur) are not deliberate to misinform, because facts and events become woolly by the effluxion of time. That such errors may occur do not deter my determination to produce this book for there is a popular saying that "it is better to try and fail than fail to try."

I have not consulted any book, manuscript and no references are attached to the work as the work is based on my childhood experiences and early adolescence of events, people and places of this God's own town – "Umu-Chukwu" or Arochukwu the land of my birth. A name which I have interpreted to mean:

"**A**rrive"
"**R**emain"
"**O**bserve"

be
"Calm"
"Hallow"
for
"Unassumption"
is the
"Key" to
"Wisdom" and
"Understanding"

George M. Onwuchekwa Esq
Monday 16th May 1994

AROCHUKWU GOLDEN YEARS

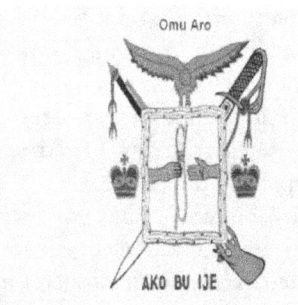

DEDICATION

Dedicated to the Arochukwu Braves (Soldiers)
Who fought gallantly, but lost their lives during the British
Colonial Invasion of Arochukwu Kingdom between AD
1901 and 1902. Their indomitable spirits keep marching on.

By George M. Onwuchekwa Esq.

(Iyiukwu-Aro)

First Published 2nd May 2000

PREFACE

In my earlier books on Arochukwu namely: "Arochukwu Marriage Custom" in 1993 and "Arochukwu Land of my Birth" in 1994, I had written about what I knew or what I remembered about what I thought I knew. In this work, however, I have not only written about what I knew, but have commented on some of the works or essays of notable historians on the ancient town of Arochukwu and the proverbial "Ibinukpabi" – the "Long-Juju". The land of God's own people ("Umu-Chukwu"). I have objectively blended my commentary, my personal knowledge with authentic oral tradition of departed Arochukwu progenitors handed down to me during my tutelage.

There is at the time of my writing, a dearth of written work on Arochukwu. Most modern historians sometimes ignore or are reluctant to emphasize some important events of Nigerian Historical Origin. History, it has been often time said, should be remembered so as to guide the present and the present in conjunction with the past should guide the future. It is not easy to come by some of the published works on Arochukwu, many of which are a Century or half-Century old and mostly out of print. It is for this reason that I have been motivated to assemble in one pamphlet or book, parts of some of the ancient and significant essays of sages both dead and living in Arochukwu Golden Years. I am grateful to my Secretary Miss Chinenye Nnorom who dutifully typed the work and as usual, my dear wife Mary Magdalen – my handy proof-reader extraordinaire.

George M. Onwuchekwa (Iyiukwu-Aro)
Festac Town
Lagos
2nd May 2000

TABLE OF CONTENTS

PREFACE
Introduction

CHAPTER ONE:
Historical Essays
Commentary

CHAPTER TWO:
Women in Politics

CHAPTER THREE:
Arochukwu and her mercenaries
Commentary

CHAPTER FOUR:
Acquired Culture
Mgbede Culture
Education and Christianity
The Culture of Secrecy

CHAPTER FIVE:
Ancestor – Worship
Reincarnation

CONCLUSION

A. His Royal Majesty -
Late Eze Kanu Oji GCON,
Eze-Aro VII
Ruled 1914 - 1987.

B. His majesty - Late Eze Kanu Oji. Eze - Aro VII with the late Eze Ibom Isii, the late Eze Ezeagwu and The Village Heads.

C. His Majesty - Late Eze Kanu Oji. Eze - Aro VII with women representative of Arochukwu villages (Inyom - Aro).

His Majesty - Late
Eze Kanu Oji, Eze - Aro VII with the present Eze as a youngman, (extreme right) - Prince Ogbonnaya Okoro (as then he was). Extreme left with his wife, is Mazi Kanu Ngwaogu, a highly educated member of the Royal family. Sitting between Eze - Aro VII and Ogbonnaya Okoro, is Her Royal Highness (HRH) Late Mary Kanu Oji, one of the wives of the Late Eze - Aro VII. Prince Ogbonnaya Okoro has since ascended the Arochukwu throne as Eze Aro VIII.

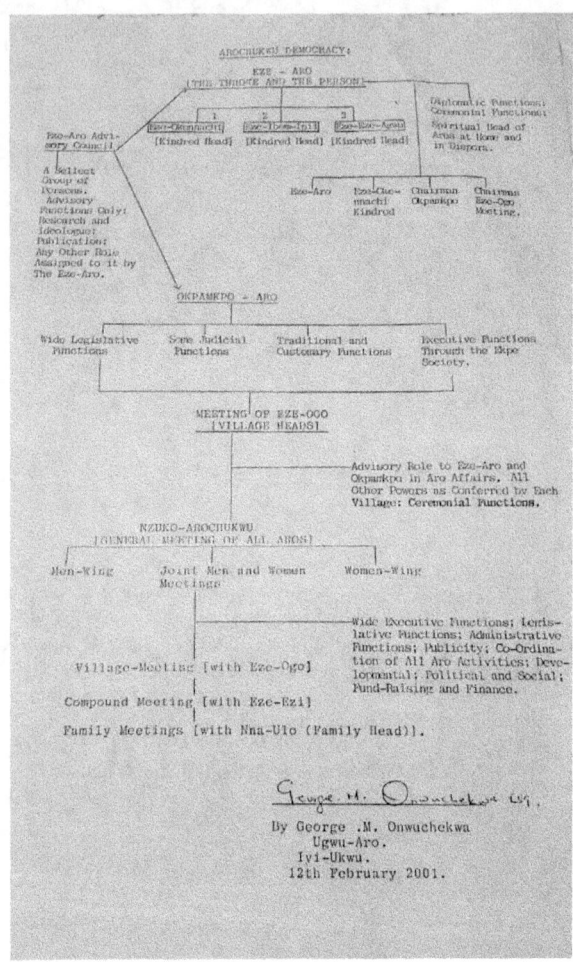

By George .M. Onwuchekwa
Ugwu-Aro.
Iyi-Ukwu.
12th February 2001.

INTRODUCTION

There is no consensus among historians as to the origin of Arochukwu Town and its people. However, every known historian who had studied and written about Arochukwu, often refer to Aros' accomplishments, intelligence, diplomacy, administrative prowess and commerce which in most cases were linked to their possession of the then famous and powerful oracle – the "Long-Juju" (Ibinukpabi) which exerted great influence over a vast territory, from the Cameroon border, Efik-land, Ibibio-land, Igbo-land, the borders of River Benue, across the River Niger to the Western Igbo Areas, the Bonny river and the entire Eastern oil-producing States of Nigeria.

It is only people with very high intellectual capacity with central administration and diplomacy that could have exerted such an influence over a vast territory at a time when there were no modern means of communication. Even today, most of the roads traversing these vast expanse of land in Nigeria are atrocious and in some cases non-existent. It was this ability, intelligence, commerce et-al that posed the greatest threat to the British colonialists in their strife to maintain political and economic dominance of Nigeria.

The rivalry in trade and economic control if not political control of the vast area of Aro dominance, brought Arochukwu on a path of head-on collision with the British Administration. This culminated in the colonial military invasion which was tagged expedition of Arochukwu between 1901 and 1902 and was said to be fiercest British colonial military engagement in Nigeria with loss of lives on both sides. The military invasion led to the near total destruction of the ancient town, its people and the severance of its trade routes and hegemony over some of the territories under the control of the Long-Juju. However, the Aros because of their superior intelligence rallied round quickly to adapt to the new order and to convert their defeat into victory in the ideological warfare that ensued thereafter and thereby, were able to preserve their central administration, and some ancient institutions.

Institutions preserved include the status of the Arochukwu Monarch (the Eze Aro). Democracy in the status of the Eze-Aro-in-Council made up of the Eze Aro, the Eze Ibom Isii, and the Eze-Ezeagwu representing the three (3) historical kindreds of Arochukwu with the Eze-Aro as Chairman and also in dual capacity representing the Oke Nnachi Kindred, which gave the Eze-Aro a casting or second vote in deliberations of the Eze-Aro-In-Council. The late Eze-Aro, Mazi Kanu Oji who ruled for over seventy three (73) years, informed me that although he had the power of second or casting vote, that in practice, he tried very much to reach compromise by carefully listening to the views of the other two Ezes and bringing to bear personally on discussion his vast knowledge of Arochukwu, its history and tradition and through which he was able in most cases to persuade the other Ezes to accept his view and to reach a compromise. He only resorted, on very few occasions reluctantly, to overrule the other two Ezes in order to postpone or adjourn deliberations for necessary consultations to be made by all parties before the final decision was reached and, in many of such cases he was proved to be right.

He said *"Anaghi achi Aro achi, kama ana eso Aro eso"* meaning "you don't rule Aro by the dictate of the Monarch, but follow the wishes and the aspirations of the generality of the Aros. Because of this tenet, the late Eze Kanu Oji was highly respected by every Aro man at home and in diaspora and also nationally and he was consulted on various national issues affecting Nigeria and had conferred on him one of the highest honours in the land – that of Grand Commander of the Order of the Niger (GCON)[1].

---

[1] See G.M. Onwuchekwa "To thine self be True" 1994 P.3

At the village level, each "Eze-Ogo" (village Eze or Head) was represented at the "Okpa-Mkpo" meeting or meeting of Eze-Aro, Eze-Ibom Isii, Eze-Ezeagwu of which the Eze-Aro was also Chairman and all village heads were members. In addition to central Administration and democracy, some Arochukwu Culture were preserved such as the marriage custom[2], system of mediation, arbitration and conciliation which harmonise the rights of disputants in marriage matters, family matters, land tenure, contract, trade, burial rites and inter-village disputes – the emphasis being on arbitration and conciliation. This was the main reason why the Aros shunned the Whiteman's Court which decision was cut and dry and in most cases did not take into account the Arochukwu culture of give and take in dispute resolution (except in criminal matters) and not winner takes all[3].

---

[2] See Arochukwu Marriage Customs 1993 by G.M. Onwuchekwa

[3] See Arochukwu Land of my Birth 1994 by G.M Onwuchekwa (pages 26 – 27 of original print)

CHAPTER ONE

HISTORICAL ESSAYS

1. SIR ALAN BURNS G. C. M. G. (History of Nigeria 8th Revised Edition 1972 –First Published 1929)

Sir Alan Burns first came to Southern Nigeria in 1912 about ten (10) years after the Arochukwu conquest of 1901 – 1902. In 1942 Sir Alan Burns acted as Governor of Nigeria. He was present in the old Court House in Tinubu Square, Lagos on January 1, 1914, when the amalgamation of the Northern and Southern Nigeria was proclaimed and was present also on October 1st 1960 at the Independence ceremony at Lagos Racecourse.

According to him:

"There must be few Africans or Europeans, who were present on both of these historic occasions[4].

Sir Alan writes:

"The Aros are held by some to be a clan of the Ibo tribe, and by others to be of an entirely different stock; however that may be, the fact remains that by their superior ability they acquired a complete ascendancy over the neighbouring Ibo Clans[5].

"With slave-dealing, however, the Government would allow no compromise, and it was necessary in 1902 to attack the powerful Aro tribe, which was still unsubdued. This tribe exerted a tremendous influence over a vast extent of Country between the Niger and the Cross-River owning to their control of an important oracle (the Long-Juju) at

---

[4] See Preface to the 6th edition "History of Nigeria" by Sir A. Burns

[5] Alan Burns History of Nigeria 8th Edition P.59

Arochukwu. The Aros were not a military race, but owed their power to their relatively great intelligence as compared with the neighbouring tribes, they seldom fought themselves, but dealt with their enemies by sending against them the warlike tribes under their influence, recompensing their mercenaries with the loot obtained from their vanquished foes."

"No dispute could be settled save by reference to the oracle........Each of the contending parties attempted to propitiate this oracle by large offerings and the party against whom judgment was pronounced was believed by his tribe to have been destroyed by the hidden power, while, in reality, he was almost invariably sold secretly into slavery[6].

"As the Aros refused to abandon these practices, a strong expedition, to which contingents from Lagos and Northern Nigeria were attached, marched to Arochukwu in converging columns and overcame all resistance. The Aros gave fresh indication of their intelligence by immediately accepting the new conditions and taking advantage of the increased trade caused by the opening up of their Country[7]".

"In 1897 the most powerful potentate in Southern Nigeria, the King of Benin, was a mere puppet in the hands of the priests and a few years later it was necessary to break up the influence of the Aros, who by the possession of a 'Long-Juju' of extraordinary power kept the surrounding Country in a state of terror and reduced the neighbouring tribes to a condition of abject submission"[8].

"......within a few years the whole of Nigeria was being administered by British Officials, aided whenever possible, by the African Chiefs and their officials. The bloody tyranny of the king of Beni, the

---

[6] See Alan Burns History of Nigeria 8th Edition P.215 and also Report on Southern Nigeria for 1902 (Colonial Reports, Annual Number 405)

[7] See Alan Burns History of Nigeria P.216

[8] See Alan Burns History of Nigeria 8th Edition P.263

malign influence of the Aros the oppression of the slave-raiding Fulani Emirs were replaced by an ordered administration which stood between the long-suffering peasantry and their hereditary tyrants"[9].

COMMENTARY:

Sir Alan Burns by his marvellous credentials had given a very good account of events as he saw, read about or was told, about the ancient Kingdom of Arochukwu and of the Arochukwu oracle (the Long-Juju or Ibinukpabi). His treatise though not in detail has given an insight into some aspects of the Golden Years of Arochukwu. However, he has trivialised some important aspects of Arochukwu history (one should excuse him). His book is of the History of Nigeria and he confesses that "It has been impossible to deal fully in a volume with every incident"[10]. However, non-inclusion of an event is different from trivialisation of an event included in his treatise – the events of 1901 – 1902 which was the British albatross.

The British invasion of Arochukwu was said to have started on 28th December 1901[11]. But, it was started in 1902 that Arochukwu was overwhelmed – by the British having been beaten in 1901 by the Aros and this led to the invasion of 1902 about which Sir Alan Burns commented at page 216 as follows: "*...a strong expedition, to which contingents from Lagos and Northern Nigeria were attached, marched to Arochukwu in converging columns and overcame all resistance.*"

It is worthy of note, that the Aros had made contact with the earlier Spanish and Portuguese traders and through such trade, had acquired military hardware and accoutrement of the time which included muskets, cannons, gunpowder and

---

[9] See Alan Burns History of Nigeria 8th Edition P.307

[10] Preface to History of Nigeria 1929

[11] See the Guardian Newspaper Saturday April 22nd 2000

ancient swords, some of them captured by the Aros in 1901 from the invading forces which were ambushed. Hundreds of these ancient swords are still at Arochukwu town in possession of families. It is also reckoned that the Sword of Colonel Gregory who is said to have led one of the expeditions was also captured and is at Arochukwu with a family. During the burial celebrations in 1987 of the late Eze Kanu Oji (the 7th Eze-Aro), numerous ancient swords (family heirlooms) although in rusty condition some of them with battered sheaths (due to lack of care), were brandished by dancers – a symbol of Arochukwu's glorious past. Old cannons dot the frontages or entrances of ancient family houses or compounds.

The British, because of the loss they suffered in 1901, came back forcefully in 1902. And, whereas the British had tried to preserve the ancient structures which they found in Northern Nigeria and in Benin City, in the case of Aro Kingdom, in their bid to destroy the Long-Juju, they destroyed almost everything in sight, artefacts, shrines, ancient houses, ancient emblems, and writing (Nsibiri) with their superior fire power and for which no reparation has been made. While carting away some heirlooms and artefacts. A surviving reminder of an ancient civilization with a writing (Nsibiri) are the drawings, patterns, symbols and creatures which are to be found on the "Ukara Loincloth" worn by Arochukwu males who have been initiated into the traditional "Ekpe-na-Mboko" society[12].

---

[12] See G.M. Onwuchekwa "Arochukwu Land of My Birth" 1st Edition 1994 P.41

CHAPTER TWO

WOMEN IN POLITICS

Although I have mentioned elsewhere the central administrative structure of Arochukwu namely: The Arochukwu Monarch, (the institution of Eze-Aro); the Eze-Aro-in-Council made up of the Eze-Aro, Eze-Ibom-Isii, and Eze Ezeagwu, the Okpamkpo (meeting of the Eze-Aro-in-Council with the village heads (Eze Ogo), no mention was made of the populace meeting for the generality of Arochukwu citizens which had undergone changes in name at one time or another, the present name being 'Nzuko Arochukwu'. There was also no mention, of the role of Arochukwu women folk in the development of Arochukwu Democracy.

It is common knowledge that the ancient town of Arochukwu was once ruled by a woman, Her Highness Nnene Mgbokwo Udo Omini[13]. Paragraph seven (7) of the 'Memorandum of Evidence on the Status of Chiefs in Arochukwu' submitted by the Ezes to Professor G. I. Jones the British Sole Commissioner dated 23rd day of May 1956, which was subsequently incorporated in the Jones Report on Chieftaincy matters in Eastern Nigeria in 1956 note the reign of this woman. The Memorandum of Evidence, whilst observing that a woman, Her Highness Nnene Mgbokwo Udo Omini at one time held the exalted position of Eze-Aro, went further to state as follows:-

> "*In the Aro constitution the influence of women was considerable. At weddings and funerals the eldest daughters (Adas) of the house, compound or village, as the case may be, wield much influence.*

---

[13] See Paragraph 7 of the Memorandum of Evidence on Status of Chiefs in Arochukwu, submitted by the Eze- Aro-In-Council to Professor G.I. Jones, Sole Commissioner 1956

Certain rites could not be performed without their consent. In the Aro council the Umu-Ada (collection of Eldest daughters) were very powerful. Cases have been recorded where they interfered with the decision of Council to the extent of countermanding suspension of orders of members or used their influence to restore peace and order on a threat of exodus of all women from the city-state[14]."

It must be appreciated that Nnene Mgbokwo Udo Omini ruled Arochukwu over a century ago and before the British invasion of Arochukwu in 1901 -1902. And, Arochukwu women had through various pressures, protests and sacrifices forced their menfolk to accord them (although reluctantly) with recognition in public affairs. It is not unlike the suffragettes in England in 1914 when the British women sought the right to vote through protests sometimes with disastrous consequence, which eventually led to women emancipation in voting matters in England[15].

This trend of women's active engagement in Arochukwu public affairs has been carried on till this day and recognition is given to Arochukwu womenfolk. A good example is the woman President of Atani Arochukwu Welfare Union, Lagos branch. And also, at the Arochukwu National level there is always a President General for the men and another President General for the women of Nzuko Arochukwu although in joint sitting of the men and women at a meeting the President General of the women wing in support both sitting side by side. The Aba Women's Riot of 1929 spilled over to Arochukwu where the womenfolk were already well organised and many incidents were recorded. It was also alleged that they participated in the Aba brouhaha.

---

[14] See 12 above.

[15] See Alan Burns History of Nigeria 8th Edition P.215

CHAPTER THREE

AROCHUKWU AND HER MERCENARIES

Many authors, notably Sir Alan Burns, J. B. Webster, A.A. Boahen, Ellen Thorps and others speak of Aro use of mercenaries in warfare.

Although mercenaries as described by these renowned authors were used by the Aros, yet Arochukwu had a standing army for local protection – for whilst mercenaries were used for outside conquests it was impossible to trust your own security to mercenaries and the Aros knew this either because of their supreme intelligence or as a benefit of hindsight.

Sir Alan Burns in his History of Nigeria stated that "The Aros were not a military race, but owed their power to their relatively great intelligence as compared with the neighbouring tribes; they seldom fought themselves, but dealt with their enemies by sending against them the warlike tribes under their influence, recompensing their mercenaries with the loot obtained from their vanquished foes[16]".

J. B. Webster and A. A. Boahen in their book "The Growth of African Civilisation"[17] gave account of the use of mercenaries by the Aros. Dr Okoi Arikpo (as he then was) recognised at least that the Akpa, one of the early Arochukwu founding fathers (Ibom Isii) had skill in warfare.

COMMENTARY

There was no doubt that the Aros made use of mercenaries to instil discipline on recalcitrant towns and tribes that defied Aro authority. However, it must be noted that mercenaries were also used to protect the life of the Aroman outside his

---

[16] See Alan Burns History of Nigeria 8th Edition P. 215

[17] The Revolutionary years West Africa since 1800 12th Impression 1976

domain as the blood of the Aroman 'Nwachukwu' child of God from Umu-Chukwu (people of God) was considered sacred.

The Aros did not trust mercenaries for the internal protection of the Aro city-state either out of their well acknowledged intelligence of as a result of hindsight. The Aros had their own great internal army. Two such regiments were said to have been led in 1901 and 1902 by two great Aro sons Udonsi Ajah and Okoro Ndem among others and they acquitted themselves creditably.

The suggestion of Sir Alan Burns that 'the Aros were not a military race' was merely a case of the victor writing the history. When it came to the question of self-defence of the homestead, it was an all Arochukwu affair.

Even when mercenaries were used for external aggression, the Aros were the scouts and intelligence men and supplied the logistics to guide and lead the mercenaries who most of the time neither knew where they were going nor how to get there. Aros are good scouts. Even when the Nigerian Boys Scout movement was formed it is noteworthy that an Aro youth (my maternal uncle) late Daniel Okoro[18] was among the twenty-four (24) Nigerian Boys Scout who represented Nigeria in the 1929 Jamboree in England. His younger brother Mazi Jonathan Obom Okoro who only died in April 2000 was a soldier in West African Frontier Force and based in Sierra Leone during the Second World War.

A city-state[19], like Arochukwu could not entrust its defence to no-stakeholders. Arochukwu was a city-state not in terms of surrounding walls or moat, but the Aros allowed less offensive and friendly towns to immediately surround Arochukwu, for the purpose of farming and fishing. These

---

[18] See "The Lady" A Biography of Lady Oyinkan Abayomi by Folarin Coker 1987 P.71

[19] See Aro submission to Jones Commission 1956 and also J. B. Webster the growth of African Civilisation 12th Impression P. 208

towns are to the North – Ututu and Ihechiowa; to the east – the Itu villages of what is now known as South-West Calabar up to the town of Atani Anayom; and to the South by Obotme and Ikpe and the peripheral or fringe towns now in the Akwa Ibom State. These towns acted as buffer-zones, early warning system of human shield or barricade.

The Editor of Nigeria Magazine D.W. MacRow writes:

"Then came the period when the Aro intelligence was brought into full play. This was the period of welding together of the different peoples – Ibo, Ibibio, Akpa...... into a homogenous whole and the blending of their culture into a peculiar one".

"Akpa communities, skilled in the art of warfare, straddled along the main route to the north. Some of them held the eastern flank, some commanded the southern approaches. The weakest, numerically of the Akpa communities guarded the western flank from where attack was least expected. The Akpa thus formed a strong hedgehog against hostile approaches." [20]

The Akpas were part of the homogenous whole of Arochukwu and formed one of the three Kindreds (Ibom-Isii). The other Kindred being Okennachi (the Kindred that selects the Eze-Aro from its royal house) and the Ezeagwu. Apart from the exploits of Akpa Warriors, there is evidence that after Arochukwu had become a homogenous whole, braves (soldiers) were selected from all the Kindreds, this explains the positon of Atani Village a border Arochukwu Village which is made up of the three (3) Kindreds, but originally, was a military encampment.

Although I do not entirely agree with the views of the late Dr Okoi Arikpo – the great Anthropologist as to the origins

---

[20] See Nigeria Magazine No 53 1957 P.107

of the Aros, as asserted in his 1957 Lugard Lectures entitled 'WHO ARE THE NIGERIANS?'[21], Dr Arikpo at least appreciated that the Aros had military bite[22].

"They resorted to the use of mercenaries only when their skill was resisted, for punitive purposes…."[23]

For defensive purposes the Aros looked inwards. It is noteworthy that the two greatest commanders who defended Arochukwu during the 1967 – 1970 Nigerian Civil War namely: Colonel S.O. Uwakwe (Rtd) and Lt. Colonel Anthony Eze (Rtd) were both Arochukwu sons. They ensured that the Federal Troops did not enter Arochukwu town until the end of the hostilities. These brave commanders who were retired from the Nigerian Army at the cessation of hostilities in 1970 would have been great generals in the Nigerian Army, but for the Civil War which pitched them on the Biafran side.

It is admitted though, that the Aros are not many in present day Nigerian Army, Airforce or Navy unlike some other communities in Nigeria to whom the military presents the first choice of a career. The reason why the Aros shun the present day army can be traced to the fact that the Aros having used mercenaries, do not want to be the mercenary of anybody. Perhaps it was this reluctance to be recruited into the British or Whiteman's army after the Arochukwu conquest that led Sir Alan Burns and other writers of his vintage to wrongly conclude that the Aros were no fighting people. Obviously the Aros were not savages, head-hunters, bushmen, mercenaries or load carriers, but had an ordered society with good central and local government.

---

[21] See Lugard Lecture 1957 P.18

[22] See Lugard Lecture 1957 P.18

[23] See Nigeria Magazine No 53 1957 P.112.

The Arochukwu forefathers were adept in diplomacy and commerce. The Aros never brooked the breaking of treaties and agreements and were in those days prepared to go to war for the sanctity of Agreements – (treaties and Agreements) not reduced into parchments or documents, but which were sealed by the exchange of daughters in marriage. Arochukwu forefathers were upright and trusted by all who came in contact with them – particularly their allies in commerce and war.

CHAPTER FOUR

ACQUIRED CULTURE

Although Arochukwu town was physically defeated by the British conquest of 1901 – 1902, it was clear that the spirit of the Aroman was not defeated in 1902. In fact, the so-called destruction of the Long-Juju (Ibinukpabi), even by the British account, was finally eradicated in 1912 and not in 1902 – that is to say ten (10) years after the conquest. This shows the resilience and spiritual doggedness of the Aros[24]. The indomitable spirit of the Aros, led them to preserve most of their ancient civilised culture – the Mgbede culture, Arochukwu Marriage Custom[25], democracy, burial rites the libation and breaking of Kolanuts, the Ekpe society, culture of secrecy etc.

MGBEDE CULTURE

The Mgbede culture is as old as Arochukwu itself. Although originally a borrowed culture during the inter-tribal war years, it became deeply rooted and was sanitised by the Aros immediately after the war which established the Arochukwu Kingdom[26] Mgbede culture was the culture of putting young maidens in fattening-rooms to groom them and make them supple for marriage. In those days, a young woman's partly-exposed body at the Ikeji celebration (New Yam Festival) was

---

[24] Nigeria Magazine (D.W. Macrow) No.53. 1957 p.115 Paragraph 2

[25] See "Arochukwu Marriage Custom" 1993 by George M. Onwuchekwa Esq

[26] See Arochukwu Land of My Birth 1st Ed 1994 Pgs 36 - 37

the eloquent evidence of her pedigree and parental nurture, which she exhibited with pride if full blossomed[27].

The braves of war (soldiers) were rewarded with beautiful slaves – mainly the female captives of war, as property. The beautiful slave girls were retained whilst the less fair ones were sold into slavery because Arochukwu were regarded as a pure race; the (Umu-Chukwu) children of God and only the best were good enough for Aro. These captive girls part of the spoils of war were found in spite of their primitive condition to be fatter, supple and rotund than the girls – the city dwellers of Arochukwu. Rather than take these girls as slaves, the braves (beneficiaries) treated them with utmost respect and care, brandishing them about wherever they went and made them visible in his presence and at every public occasion, giving them the best food, clothing and ornaments.

This change of behaviour by their menfolk provoked jealousy, envy and in some cases outright hatred from the homebred Aro-wives, but violence towards these newly acquired wives were averted by the timely intervention and strength of character of their husbands. However, as time went on, many mothers insisted that their daughters must be presented to their husbands on the Eke-Ekpe day, to exhibit her virgin and well nurtured plump daughter , in order to confer a high status on her in her marital home. This in fact worked. And here started a culture of fattening-room and the dancing of the young maidens at Eke-Ekpe day at the Ikeji (New Yam) celebration before handing her over to her husband. This began a culture of public wedding or public celebration of marriage which conferred stronger marital status on the new wife.

It must be mentioned that only girls who are virgo-intacta (virgins) that come out to dance at the Amaikpe Square. Others who undergo the fattening room grooming, but fail the test of purity and chastity (although in the hands of their

---

[27] Ibid 36-37

would-be husbands) are taken to their husband's home via another ceremony. They did not dance at the Amaikpe Square for fear that they would be smothered by the spirit of the ancestors (Ndichie) said to be the spirits of departed Aro heroes[28].

EDUCATION AND CHRISTIANITY

As Sir Alan Burns stated in his History of Nigeria[29] after the Aros had been overcome by the British Expedition or conquest:

"The Aros gave fresh indication of their intelligence by immediately accepting the new conditions and taking advantage of the increased trade caused by opening up of their country."

I must state that at first, there was great reluctance and mistrust, but after 1912[30], the supposed actual demise of the Long-Juju (Ibinukpabi), the Aros turned to Education and Christianity, but in doing so however, did not neglect or jettison most of their civilised culture.

By early 1920s, Arochukwu had in its fold many educated men and women who had passed through one College or another, established by the Missionaries. Many of whom were trained teachers who were principal staffs and Headmasters of Missionary and other schools. To mention, but a few: late Dr Alvan Ikoku, late Mazi S.O. Nwangoro, late Mazi Ogwuma, late Mazi Nwafor Udo, late Madam Alice Udo, late

---

[28] Note that not all Aro departed souls are deemed to be Ndichie, no matter their age before death. Ndichie are spiritual patriarchs according to Arochukwu standards.

[29] See Alan Burns History of Nigeria 8th Edition P. 216

[30] See Nigeria Magazine No 53 1957 P.115.

Mazi Emmanuel Oti, late Teacher Moses Onwuchekwa, late Mazi T.K. Utchey, late Mazi Jack Ogbonnaya, late Mazi Sampson Okoro, late Barrister Edward Kanu Uku, late Dr Chima Oji. Arochukwu produced also by early 1920s and before the outbreak of the Second World War, educated and ordained Pastors, Reverends, Catechists and other missionaries among who were late Rev. Uwakwenta, late Rev. Ijoma, late Rev. Nwana, late Rev. P.B. Onwuchekwa, late Rev. Alfred Anicho, late Rev. Inyama. Aro teachers and Pastors who were mainly of the Church of Scotland Mission (now the Presbyterian Church of Nigeria) except Rev. Nwana who was of the Methodist Mission at Umuahia and Rev. Ebel Onwuchekwa who was of the Qua-Iboe Mission near Aba, were posted to head schools and Churches all over the land of their former mercenaries. Examples include Abiriba, Ohafia, Abam, Eda, and the entire area now part of Cross-River and Akwa-Ibom states, which under colonial administration were grouped under the old Arochukwu District with headquarters at Aro.

By 1932 Dr Alvan Ikoku had established in Arochukwu town the famous Aggrey Memorial College - the only African Secondary School east of River Niger which was both recognised and approved by the colonial administration. Its establishment was at a time when Secondary School education was the preserve of the Government and missionaries. Late Rev. Inyama had founded Schools in Okigwe (now in Imo State) and late Mazi T.K. Utchey had established Empire 'V' School Aba, Cunardia School Port Harcourt and Jubilee School Arochukwu. Late Mazi Peter Nwana had written the first Igbo literature book 'OMENUKO'. Aros in diaspora were to follow afterwards with the establishment of Iheme Memorial Grammar School Aro-Ndizuogu, Aro Ndizuogu National High School and at Ihiala.

In 1999, Arochukwu could count for not less than twenty-five (25) professors in addition to scores of lecturers at varying grades (dead and alive) who serve or had served in various

Nigerian Universities and Overseas. This shows to what extent the Aros have imbibed education and religion, which in fact was their second nature.

THE CULTURE OF SECRECY

The strongest culture preserved by the Aros after the British expedition of 1901 to 1902 is the culture of secrecy. There is a saying in Arochukwu that "Aro anaghi ezu-nzi, Aro anaghi, Agba – ama" in other words, the Aro man does not steal and the Aro man does not expose the thief. This literally means that an Aro man minds his business. So strong is this culture, that in the past, it was very difficult for an outsider or even a non-well-placed Aro man, to obtain information about Aro, its history, its people, and its places. It was like squeezing water out of a stone. By mere fact of asking certain questions, your motive became suspicious and if you are not careful, you were, you are taken to be a spy and immediately reported to the elders. Once reported you became 'persona non grata.'

It is not unexpected that the Aros should adopt a culture of secrecy – after all, the 'Long Juju' was the most guarded Aro secret and it was a capital offence or at least an offence for which a citizen could be ostracised and perhaps sold into slavery for unwittingly divulging to strangers and even to non-well placed Aro men the secrets connected with the Ibinukpabi (Long Juju). This explains why the Aros as intelligent and educated as they were and are, have written little about Aro history or for that matter on other aspects of the legendary Aro man.

Most of the books on Arochukwu are written by the colonial masters, indifferent academicians and interested outsiders some of whom may be antagonistic. No wonder that various aspects of Aro history have been distorted and our great oral tradition passed down from our forefathers have been allowed to rest with the ancestors.

I was privileged to have grown up in the midst of elders, great and grand uncles and aunties and their friends from other villages and kindreds of Aro some of whom were octogenarians or nonagenarians at the time I was growing up and who actually participated in the struggles of 1901 -1902. Moreover, most of Arochukwu early educated men of the 1920s and 1930s were well known to me and they had explained matters to me under strict discipline[31].

---

[31] Historically the Aro man believed that the earth was divided into two – the Aros and the non-Aros, and whoever was not an Aro man, no matter his wealth and sophistication is a bushman. See also: late Mazi T.K. Utchay "*Nwa Aro Icho, Mkpola icho.*"

CHAPTER FIVE

ANCESTOR – WORSHIP

The ancient Aros, revered their ancestors (the Ndichie). The Ndichie or forefathers were the departed heroes – particularly the founders of the Arochukwu Kingdom and other departed persons who were publicly acknowledged to have rendered selfless services or had distinguished themselves in commerce, diplomacy, settlement of disputes, the arts, culture and tradition of the land. Ndichie were regarded as spirits and were the intermediaries between God and the Aros. Not every dead elder or person was looked upon as Ndichie or Ndichie-Aro.

The Aros in the performance of their daily activities (private or public) invoked the spirit of the Ancestors to intercede between them and God on High (Obasi-di-nelu). This was observed in the breaking of Kolanut, pouring of the libation, or rubbing of the white chalk (Nzu). The Aros believed strongly in God the almighty, or God on High (Obasi-di-nelu). "Ndichie" were mainly intermediaries. There is a saying in Arochukwu "I know my father and my father knows our God". Father here means lineal ancestors (Ndichie). God here must be distinguished from the Christian God.

God almighty was placed highest and was acknowledged as the creator of the universe and He was called by such hallowed names as "Chukwu" (God); "Chineke" (God of Creation); "Obasi-di-nelu" (God most High) etc. The Aros regarded themselves as the children of God (Umu-Chukwu), and the name "Arochukwu" derives from "Umu-Chukwu" or the chosen people of God. There is some similarity between the Aros and the Jews and, there is a school of thought which believes that the Aros were descendants of the Jews because of their claim as the chosen people of God and their acknowledged intelligence.

Various shrines, "Awada", "Ulo-nta", landmarks and monuments (temples), were erected and dedicated for the worship of the almighty God, where prayers and offerings were made. The Aros unlike many other Nigerian tribes did not worship the idols, god of fire, stone, the sun, mood, god of thunder and others. The Aros saw no reason to worship any other god since they were merely places of worship where prayers and sacrifices were offered to God in the Old Testament fashion, through the "Ndichie." This was similar to how the Jews acknowledged the God of their ancestors or fathers - Abraham, Isaac and Jacob.

Most of the shrines and temples were destroyed by the British during the Arochukwu conquest of 1901 – 1902, in their desperate quest to destroy the Arochukwu Long-Juju (Ibinukpabi) in any visible form whether related or unrelated. How could they have told the difference? A few surviving (or in some cases refurbishments) of the ancient temples and places of worship are the "Awada-Aro", "Ulo-nta Ndi-Okoroji". "Nkuma-Amaikpe" (the Stones of Union); "Ukwu-Offor", "Oji-Ogo" (the great Iroko trees among others).

Prayers and offering were made by the Aros through the ancestors. But the Aros acknowledge the supremacy of one deity known as God on High (Obasi-di-nelu) by calling on his name, before asking the ancestors to intercede. A usual prayer followed this order – "Obasi di nelu", "Ndichie – Aro"….etc. In other words, God on High, Aro Ancestors….etc. before other praises or supplications are made such as for good health of the family, prosperity in trade, good harvest, protection on a long journey, safe delivery of a child, as the case may be. Kola nut is broken, libation is poured and white chalk is broken and sprinkled as a mark of respect and in some cases animals are sacrificed depending on the occasions or mood.

The ancient Aro man never prayed for the downfall of an enemy (except in war) rather, he would pray to God to ward-off or neutralise the evil machinations of the enemy and for co-existence in peace with others. They believed in the principle of "live and live". Phrases such as "egbe bere, ugo bere" were used often, to highlight this principle. This principle made the Aros the most travelled Nigerians and the most settled in areas outside their kingdom in the whole of the former Eastern Nigeria.

REINCARNATION:

The Ancient Aro – man believed in reincarnation, which is the rebirth of a soul in a new body particularly of an ancestor. On the birth of a child, brainstorming takes place within the larger family to identify which among the ancestors has reincarnated. A conclusion is always arrived at, by the pronouncement of the family sages, after a careful observation of the supposed likeness and assumed mannerism of the baby.

So strong was the relationship between an ancient Aro-man and his ancestors, and reincarnation, that the Aros buried their deceased relatives in the family house, within the family premises, compound or family plantation. If a deceased relation had no house of his own and had to be buried in a plot of family land, an effort was made to put a roof over that grave at the relation's earliest convenience (perhaps to protect the body from rain and sun). This practice still subsists amongst many Aros.

It was a taboo in Arochukwu to bury a deceased Aro-man in a foreign or strange place. Exception however, were made in those days, in the case of young children or those deemed to be social outcasts or alleged to be smothered by the "Ndichie" or whose affliction prior to death was attributed to the visitation or punishment from god. Some strangers were buried at the small government cemetery at Baraki[32] or in other cases were thrown into the forbidden forest ("Osisi-mkparimkpa") habited by hyena and other wild animals.

---

[32] See Arochukwu Land of My Birth 1st Ed 1994 Pgs 25-27

Some of our ancestral practices such as the breaking of the kolanut and the libation together with the incantation associated with same have provoked argument as to whether or not these practices should be retained in the present Christian dominated town.

Those who advocate retaining these customs argue that it was these ancestral practices and fears associated with "Ndichie" and their powers that in the years gone by helped to rid Aro society, of heinous crimes and despicable social vices. Many of them have argued for adaptation or blending of some of the ancestral practices to make them a stable part of Aro social heritage; in other words they desire to see a marriage of the religious culture (Canon Law) with ancestral practices on the basis that no nation should jettison its positive ancestral cultural practices and values in the name of acquired religion. Regardless of opinion, or religious persuasion it is clear from the current practices and habits of the Aros that libation and the associated prayer to the spirit of Ndichie will remain for a long time to come.

CONCLUSION

As we approach the Centenary Celebration of the British Invasion of the ancient city-state of Arochukwu (1901 – 1902), in AD 2001 – 2002, it is necessary to remind all Aros of our rich history and the accomplishments of our progenitors because such history had fashioned our present and the knowledge of our history and present will determine our future within the context of the present realities in Nigeria.

It is time that we tell ourselves the truth about ourselves – the whole truth and nothing but the truth. It is time we see ourselves as we really are and it is time we begin (if we so wish) to recover our lost glory.

Not glory in the sense of slave trade, not glory in the sense of domination of other clans and tribes, not glory in arrogance and self-delusion the "Nwa-mba ovia" syndrome[33], with an air of misplaced self-esteem, but glory in dignity, glory in hard work, glory in upholding the truth, glory in discipline, glory in shunning evil, glory in upholding the civilised elements of our culture, glory in political, economic and social progress and glory in sustaining a strong dignified and respected monarchy as the epitome of Arochukwu culture and tradition.

I conclude with the words of William Shakespeare's 'COMEDY OF ERRORS':

"We come into this world like brother and brother and now let us go hand in hand not one before another."

We must go hand in hand in the pursuit of truth, common goals with other Nigerian citizens, and common destiny as Aro citizens.

---

[33] See Arochukwu Land of My Birth 1st Ed 1994 Pg 2

An American poet, Langston Hughes wrote the following lines:

"We have tomorrow
Bright before us
Like a flame

Yesterday, a night-gone thing.
A sun—down name.

And dawn today.
Broad arch above the road we came
We march".

George M. Onwuchekwa Esq
(Iyi-Ukwu Aro)
Lagos
2nd May 2000.

THE OKENNACHI KINDRED

DEDICATION
Dedicated to the Nde-Agor youths,
Men and women of yesteryears,
today and future generations.

FROM THE EYE AND EAR
OF
George M. Onwuchekwa Esq.
(Ugwu-Aro)

First Published Monday 7th April 2008

INTRODUCTION

The Arochukwu Kingdom is made up of three kindreds namely:
  i. The Okennachi
  ii. Ibom Isii and
  iii. Ezeagwu (together with Umunna Okwaragwu)

OKENNACHI KINDRED is made up of:
  i. Utugugwu Village
  ii. Oror Village
  iii. Amankwu Village
  iv. Isimkpu Village
  v. Amangwu Village
  vi. Asaga Village
  vii. Amuvi Village
  viii. Part of Atani Village (Atani Okennachi) and
  ix. Obinkita Okennachi (Nde-Agor Compound)

IBOM ISII KINDRED is made up of:
  i. Ugwuakuma Village
  ii. Agbagwu Village
  iii. Ujari Village
  iv. Ibom Etiti (Ibom Village)
  v. Amasu Village
  vi. Amukwa Village
  vii. Oror Ibom Isii

Oror Village where the Arochukwu palace is situate, is made up of the three Arochukwu kindreds of Okennachi, Ibom Isii and Ezeagwu – with varying populations – although the Okennachi is claimed to be the dominant population of Oror.

EZEAGWU is made up of:
  i. Amanagwu Village
  ii. Obinkita Village (the original Ama-Agwu except Nde-Agor Compound) – Obinkita was a pseudonym

iii. Atani Ezeagwu (where Ezeagwu is said to be the dominant population)
  iv. Umunna Okwaragwu villages of Amoba; Ugwuavor and Ugbo

HISTORICALLY

It is undisputed that:
  i. Some of the land presently occupied by the Arochukwu kingdom was originally inhabited by Agwu and his people – the aborigines.
  ii. Agwu was not a strong Ibibio sub-tribe and frequent incursions were made into his territory by more powerful and domineering neighbours – leading to adverse consequences and loss of men and property.
  iii. A Semitic soothsayer, palmist, ornamental, fragrance and clothing merchant called NACHI or NA-KKI said to be an Egyptian Jew (part of the lost tribe of Israel after the Exodus in search of the promised land), came to settle in Agwu's domain plying his trade in the surrounding territory. It was said that he introduced the Ukara cloth. The markings and drawings on this cloth can be traced to ancient Egypt, as a form of writing (*hieroglyphics*). Na-chi or Na-kki was always welcomed to Agwu's domain because of the nature of his trade, profession and knowledge. NNACHI is a corruption or derivative of the name Na-chi or Na-kki.

On one of such invasions of Agwu's domain, Na-chi's goods were looted, but he managed to escape unhurt. He later returned with some juju men who indulged in concoction and incantation – in a bid to ward-off the enemy, however the enemy yet returned again and again with determined ferocity – leading to the death of one juju man and more looting. Na-chi realising the futility of juju as a sole instrument of warfare, decided that only a counter-force with devastating ferocity could checkmate what had become an incessant foray into

Agwu's domain. Agwu himself had become helpless and pensive.

Na-chi set out to approach his kinsman or friend (or acquaintance) a great warrior called Ackman (or Arkman) from Nubia. Nubia is a place in Northern Sudan nearest Egypt and the Red Sea.

Ackman (Arkman) was then plying his own trade at Akpa nation – near Akamkpa now in Cross-River State of Nigeria. AKUMA NNAOBI is a corruption or derivative of the name ACKMAN (or ARKMAN) NUBIA. Oral Tradition had it that both Na-chi and Arkman were really part of the Hebrew twelve lost tribes who left Egypt during mass exodus migrating to Nubia and continued in their Southern march – perhaps through Jukun in Plateau State – some to Akpa in Cross River State and others through other routes to the place now called Arochukwu Town. This particular group of Na-chi's people would have passed through Igbo speaking nations and intermarried with the local people.

It is possible that Na-chi knew Arkman before and both were from common ancestry and spoke the same Hebrew language or dialect. Nachi knew exactly where to go and look for Arkman – the ease of Arkman agreeing to go with Na-chi to wage a war, the mutuality between the duo –even though Arkman expected a reward – part of the booty of war.

Professor Okoi Arikpo, one of the greatest Nigerian Anthropologists, in his Lugard Lectures 1957 entitled "Who are the Nigerians" at page 18, stated that the Aros migrated from Jukun in Plateau State. However whether, Arkman was hired or merely invited by Na-chi to come with his troop to wage a war which had nothing to do with him, is not the issue here, since the matter under discussion, is in respect of Okennachi Kindred. It must be pointed out however, that Arkman would not have followed if Na-chi did not hold out for him some inducement or expectation of some reward – there was mutuality of confidence.

ESTABLISHMENT OF AROCHUKWU KINGDOM

Arkman came down with his braves (soldiers) mainly Akpa recruits – even though Arkman was himself not an Akpa person. He came to war with the Akpa prince called "Osim", and pitched his tent (Headquarters) at Ugwuakuma (Arkman Hill).The editor of Nigeria magazine 1957 No 53 – D.W Macrow writes at page 107 of the edition thus:

"Akpa communities skilled in the art of warfare, straddled along the main route to the north. Some of them held the eastern flank, some commanded the southern approaches, The weakest numerically of the Akpa communities guarded the western flank from where attack was least expected. The Akpa thus formed a strong hedgehog against hostile approaches."

It must be noted that Akpa people did not fight alone as Agwu's men and Na-chi's men were also involved in the war. This can explain the composition of Atani Village which consists of the three kindreds of Okennachi, Ibom Isii and Ezeagwu. Amoba, Ugbo Village, and Ugwuavor Villages which are mainly of Ezeagwu kindred (Umunna Okwara-Agwu).

DEATH OF PRINCE OSIM (The Akpa Prince)

Oral Tradition has it, that Osim, the Akpa prince volunteered to follow Arkman to war. His father, would not at first allow his son, but Arkman assured him that the young man would be safe. He further pledged that if anything happened to the young man, he would banish himself and not return home. In other words, that he would protect Osim with the last pint of his blood. So, Osim was allowed to follow Arkman – war being an adventure for youths of the time.

Towards the end of the war, a sniper's arrow struck prince Osim in the chest at the Amaoba sector and he fell. Osim was rushed out for treatment, whilst the battle continued to total and resounding victory for the alliance forces led by Arkman. Osim was then, stretchered out to the present spot at Amaikpe Square where the arrow was extracted from his chest and his Royal Blood oozed out onto the soil. The spot where Osim shed blood was marked with some stones as a mark of respect, whilst Osim was carried away for treatment in the hideout now called Oror Village he died and was buried. The Ukwu-Ovor marks his final resting place at Oror palace forecourt.

THE STONES OF UNION: (NKUMA-AMAIKPE)

I now use the modern names or appellation of NNACHI; AKUMA; NNUBI AND AGWU for these progenitors of Arochukwu for purpose of clarity.

After the final victory in the war, Akuma-Nnubi-the alliance military leader and leader of the Akpa warriors became the supreme commander of the entire territory – by virtue of his might, charisma and leadership. He became undisputedly the first king or governor or ruler of the territory now called Arochukwu. There was no distinction in terminology in these nomenclatures in those days.

There was a trial of the captives or prisoners of war at the square now known as AMAIKPE SQUARE – the first public trial in Arochukwu (I have written about this event in Arochukwu: Land of My Birth 1994 - please consult).

After Osim had died, Akuma Nnubi because of the pledge he had given Osim's father could not return to the Akpa tribe, although Oral tradition has it, that some of his men joyfully returned to their territory with their loot or spoils of war. Nnachi asked Akuma Nnubi to hand over to him the prize of victory and to relocate instead to the Headquarters of his military up the hill since Nnachi had compensated or propitiated him adequately from the spoils of war (including women) in accordance with their agreement and honour.

To this, Akuma agreed on the condition that Nnachi should come down to live near Osim's grave to look after it.

Nnachi agreed and Akuma voluntarily handed over the prize of victory to Nnachi and Nnachi moved down from his hill (Utugugwu) to the place now called Oror the seat of Arochukwu kingdom. This marks the end of Akuma's reign and the beginning of Nnachi's hegemony or rule which, in time metamorphosed into Oke-Nnachi kindred of Oror Village as many of Nnachi's kith and kin joined him at Oror.

THE MAKING OR EVOLUTION OF AROCHUKWU KINGDOM

(THE SACRIFICE AND THE STONES OF UNION)

Although Akuma had handed over the victory prize to Nnachi, yet the relationship amongst the three kindred was precarious. Nnachi was only able to hold his own because of the support and military might of Akuma Nnubi and the Ibom Isii. Agwu's domain was simmering, and conflicting rumours emerging from the domain points to Agwu and his eldest son's conflict. But, as time went by, the rumour became a reality, as the first son of Agwu – his full name was Agwu-Nwa-Agwu, escaped justice in the hands of his father with his wives and few loyalists (his immediate family). He pitched his tent behind Ibom Etiti (Ibom) for refuge (the present day Amanagwu village). Agwu the father had alleged that his son insulted him in his household and domain and needed to answer for his offence. An offence which if proven could, in those days, merit banishment or slavery but the prince's life would be spared.

Agwu demanded that Ibom should hand Agwu-Nwa-Agwu over to him, a demand Ibom refused to acknowledge. The event provoked a serious diplomatic incident between Agwu (father) and Ibom Isii under Akuma Nnubi, and the whole episode was degenerating into armed conflict between the duo but for the timely intervention of Nnachi who brokered peace between the two kindreds being a mutual friend of both parties. He achieved this using his wealth of experience, his negotiating ability and diplomatic prowess. This culminated into the signing and sealing of no violence or non-aggression pact or treaty by all the parties namely Nnachi, Akuma Nnubi and Agwu. The venue was at Amaikpe at the spot Osim the prince shed his blood. A white sheep (lamb) symbolising peace was buried at the spot whilst the three progenitors clutched hands over the peace offering and swore that no group should ever again attack, kill or molest or be hostile in anyway against any other group. They killed a Ram and ate as part of the ceremony.

Nnachi as chief negotiator was given the head of the ram in addition to other meat given to him; Akuma was given the jaw of the ram together with other meat given to him; and Agwu was given a portion of meat. Hence, as of today, whenever a live animal is slaughtered and shared in common, the Eze Aro represented by Nnachi's group takes the head, and Eze-Ibom Isii takes the jaw. Bigger stones were then assembled at the spot where Osim shed his blood, where the white lamb was buried and the non-aggression treaty was sealed.

This is what is called the stones of union "Nkuma-Amaikpe". And at the Eke-Ekpe Aro celebration, every masquerade is expected to pay homage to the spot. This dear brothers and sisters, is the beginning of Arochukwu City State (or Town) as we know it today.

THE COMING INTO PROMINENCE OF OKE NNACHI
(The First son of Nnachi)
AND
THE EVOLUTION OF OKE NNACHI KINDRED

Some years after the Arochukwu pact, Nnachi became ill and sent his first son Okezie or Oke to represent him in the kindreds' caucus with Akuma Nnubi and Agwu. He became so prominent and presided on behalf of his father and showed that he had learnt much from his father Nnachi. So when Nnachi died, Akuma placed his hands on Oke's head and he was declared Eze-Aro in place of his late father. Oke lived and reigned for a long time – became more prominent in resolving disputes and was master of diplomacy. He was generally well accepted by the other kindreds and in no time, his name and fame became a household name. Thus evolved Oke Nnachi and his people (Oke Nnachi Kindred) the other two being Ibom Isii and the Eze Agwu.

When Akuma Nnubi died, there was a smooth transition of power within Ibom Isii kindred. Nnachi died first, and there was also a smooth transition to his son Oke. But this was not so in the case of Eze-Agwu kindred – because Agwu-Nwa-Agwu - the first son, who would have succeeded his father was on voluntary exile to his new domain – Amanagwu and moreso, the "Ovi-Agwu" shrine heirloom of Agwu was at Ndi-Otuu Obinkita – the father's homestead where his younger brother lived – who by virtue of occupying the Agwu family home, claimed still to represent Agwu the father.

And Agwu-Nwa-Agwu who had by now created his own village of Amanagwu (Ama-Agwu) could not abandon his new and prosperous domain to return home to Obinkita for fear that his father's spirit will smother him. Because of the conflicting claims of the two sides of Agwu family, for centuries, Eze-Agwu kindred did not have an Eze-Eze-Agwu until 1946.

In 1946, Mazi Okoro-Nwa-Okoro the Eze Ndi-Otuu compound of Obinkita Village – the aborigines of

Arochukwu, who was by virtue of his position, also Eze-Obinkita village was ill and did not receive adequate financial support from his Obinkita Village relations and subjects, instead his brethren from Amanagwu – particularly, Mr Alvan Ikoku (as he was then) the founder of Aggrey Memorial College, gave Mazi Okoro financial support and succour. And, in fact, sent him to a hospital owned by the Scottish Missionaries at Itu Town (now in Akwa Ibom State). It is generally believed that the financial assistance given by the Amanagwu relations was with a pre-condition. Moreover, the Obinkita Elders did not attend meetings convened by Mazi Okoro-Nwa-Okoro as the Eze Obinkita, because of a disagreement between them.

Mazi Okoro was angered and severely embittered by this unwholesome attitude of his Obinkita relations and subjects. On one fateful day in 1946, towards evening, Mazi Okoro came to see my father – Teacher Moses Onwuchekwa – one of the few people in Obinkita who still respected him and gave him some financial assistance but not as much money as he received from Amanagwu – particularly from Alvan Ikoku. He refused to come into the veranda. My father was very surprised but glad to see him as everyone thought he was still at the hospital in Itu Town. He angrily informed my father that he had that morning, taken the "Ovor-Agwu" to Mazi Uror's house at Amanagwu as they the first son (Okpara). My father exclaimed in disbelief and asked him why. He said that since Obinkita did not want him to rule them, "let some other person rule them" – in reference to the attitude of the village elders towards him. He left almost immediately.

My father sent me to call Mazi Obnonnaya Anicho from Nde-Okoro (Ama-Ede) and his neighbour Mazi Ojim-Okwara (father of Bending) Mazi Anicho Nwosu another elder from Nde-Akwere (Ezi Nna Kwa) and, on my way back, I informed Mazi Okoronkwo (father of Ukwu Okoronkwo) and Mazi Okereke Abaa at Ndechioka. The elders assembled in my father's house as requested since they had mutual respect for one another. After the usual Arochukwu pleasantries of kola nuts etc. my father said in Igbo language "awo anaghi agba oso ehihie ne-fu" meaning in short, a grave emergency.

After their deliberations, all the elders trooped out to see Mazi Okoro, who then I was told, used the opportunity to castigate them. I was not there with the elders as I was attending to other chores. It was therefore this incident and several meetings with the Okennachi and Ibom Isii kindreds in the same year 1946 which united the Agwu kindred and the emergence of Eze-Eze-Agwu in 1946. Alvan Ikoku was always quoting what I now know was taken from America, during their war of Independence – "No taxation without representation."

OKENNACHI KINDRED AND ITS MEETINGS

Oke Nnachi ascended the throne of his father – (Nnachi) when his father joined his ancestors. And pursuant thereto, replaced his father as the bona fide Eze-Aro of Arochukwu Kingdom. No one knows exactly when the meeting of Okennachi kindred began – perhaps they met informally as a domestic meeting of Oke with his brothers and eventually after each successive reign metamorphosed into a full-blown kindred meeting. However, I must categorically state that I attended four of Okennachi kindred meetings – as a fledgling young boy accompanying Teacher Moses Onwuchekwa in the early 1940's (carrying his bag containing writing materials and his umbrella). I was made to sit down by his feet and listen. Many times when I lost concentration or dozed-off, the knuckles of his right hand cracked my head. At home if I failed to mention at least five names of the elders who attended a particular meeting, I received more cracks on my head. Perhaps, fear of punishment made me to remember the events but not the dates of the meetings I attended.

My first Okennachi meeting was at Utugugwu Village (Utuga-Ugwu- the hillside) it was in the early 1940s. Those present that I remembered were: Mazi Kanu Oji (the Eze Aro), Mazi Okereke Izuogu of Amankwu Village; Rev Alfred Anicho of Amuvi Village, my father Teacher Moses Onwuchekwa who acted as the secretary (Nde-Agor Compound); Mazi Imo (Oror Village); Mazi Okoruga of Utugugwu Village; Mazi Okereke said to have worked in the office of the white District Officer – Utugugwu Village; Mazi Okereke – father of Kanu Okereke of Amangwu Village; and Mazi Idei from Oror Village etc.

My second Okennachi meeting also in the early 1940's was at Amangwu Village. Those present were:
a. Mazi Kanu Oji – the Eze Aro (Oror Village)
b. Mazi Imo, Oror Village
c. Rev. Alfred Anicho – Amuvi Village
d. Teacher Moses Onwuchekwa (Nde-Agor Compound)

e. Mazi Okereke Izuogu – Amankwu Village
f. Mazi Okereke Okwara – Amankwu Village
g. Mazi Okereke – Amangwu (with his young son – Kanu)
h. Mazi Chiori – Amangwu Village
i. Mazi Obasi Onwuchekwa (Nna-Obasi) Nde-Agor compound and others

My third Okennachi meeting was at Amankwu held at the residence of Mazi Okereke Okwara in early 1940s.

Present were:
a. Mazi Kanu Oji (Eze Aro) – Oror
b. Mazi Imo – Oror
c. Teacher Moses Onwuchekwa – Nde Agor
d. Mazi Obasi Onwuchekwa (Nna-Obasi) Nde-Agor
e. Mazi Anicho Anyakoha – Amankwu
f. Mazi Okereke Izuogu – Amankwu
g. Rev. Alfred Anicho – Amuvi
h. Mazi Okereke – Utugugwu
i. Many others whose names I cannot immediately recall.

Suffice to say the meeting was well attended.

My fourth Okennachi meeting was at Nde-Agor compound. My father was then transferred and was the Head Master of Abiriba Church of Scotland Mission School and I was with my maternal uncle who was a school teacher at Amodu Mission School at Ututu Town. I knew that my father was coming home to Aro that Easter and I left Ututu to come and assist him with errands. We arrived at Arochukwu the same day – I arriving before him.

Shortly after he had arrived, Mazi Avoime Okoro who was now representing Nde-Agor and Obinkita Village in Arochukwu Council came in to welcome my father. He did not allow him to settle down but told him that he was happy that my father arrived as the Okennachi meeting was to be held in our compound (Nde-Agor compound) that afternoon. He discussed with my father the provisional arrangement he made. My father thereupon produced some money and I was sent to call Sunday Ogbealu and Sunday Okoroafor who were now sent to Amaikpe market (Amaikpe was then a daily market). The duo of Sunday Ogbealu and Sunday Okoroafor brought back a dried hind-leg and front-leg of bush meat followed with Edda people who carried jars of palm wine (Itotu-mmayi). In the meantime, the young boys of the compound were asked to gather chairs from every house in the compound and arrange same at Mazi Obasi Onwuchekwa's parlour – downstairs. De-Avoime also told my father that Mazi Obasi Onwuchekwa, who had informed him of the meeting to be held in our compound some time ago, was suddenly sent for, from the plantation to douse a dispute which could escalate if he was not present but that he was expected but not returned yet.

The meeting was well attended. Present were:
a. Mazi Kanu Oji (Eze-Aro) Oror Village
b. Mazi Imo (Oror Village)
c. Mazi Idei (Oror Village)
d. Mazi Okereke Izuogu (Amankwu Village)
e. Mazi Okereke Okwara (Amankwu Village)
f. Mazi Alfred Anicho (Amuvi Village)
g. Mazi Okereke (Utugugwu Village)
h. Teacher Sunday Oji (Atani Village)
i. Mazi Avoime Okor (Nde-Agor Compound)
j. Teacher Moses Onwuchekwa (Nde-Agor)
k. Etc.

Something inspiring happened that day which is still indelibly imprinted in my mind. As the meeting was about to rise, Mazi Job Okoro returned. He saw some people gathering at Nna Obasi's house and he came in to know what was going on. He saw Eze Kanu Oji; De Avoime, my father and others. He knew everybody and in his usual charismatic and friendly manner went around and shook hands and or hugged everybody.

Mazi Job then invited everybody to his house as the meeting had closed. I once again, with the assistance of others carried chairs from Nna-Obasi's house to Mazi Job's house.

Mazi Job produced a full bottle of Gordon gin, two bottles of Tenant beer, a tin of gem biscuits, some pepper fruits (Mmimi) and garden eggs (anara or ikete) and handed them over to De Avoime who proceeded to present them to the gathering.

When people were already going away, outside, someone noticed Mazi Obasi returning home from his plantation trip. Eze Aro came out to greet him and others followed. He said to Eze-Aro that "my people cannot stand outside to greet me." He said that he had discussed the meeting with Eze-Aro and made frantic efforts to return so as to meet the meeting. He ordered everybody back to his parlour. It was a period in Arochukwu history when people respected elders and so Eze-Aro ordered everybody back to Mazi Obasi's house. Mazi Obasi called his son Oguikpe with whom he had travelled and returned and whispered into his ear. Oguikpe brought a jute bag containing two very large hind legs of dried bush meat and Mazi offered one through my father to Eze-Aro. Eze-Aro ordered that the meat should be divided according to village and compounds represented at the meeting to take away (Ngwugwu). The meat was so chunky that villages took home large pieces and smiled home. This sense of camaraderie within the kindred as exemplified by the generosity of our elders made a strong impression on me.

I must state that this Nde-Agor meeting was the last meeting of the Okennachi kindred I attended for about thirty years because of schooling, working and finally travelling overseas in search of the proverbial Golden Fleece. At the period of the said above meetings, even though my father – Teacher Moses Onwuchekwa acted as Secretary, yet minutes were not read and adopted as in modern meetings. He was merely asked to remind the meeting of decisions taken at the last meeting. Minutes were to my knowledge not signed and were brief.

Eze Kanu Oji the Eze Aro was the motivating spirit behind Okennachi meeting as he needed to consult his brothers on many issues affecting Arochukwu or whenever the white D.O. or Resident in Calabar wanted to speak to the Aros at Barracks or at Amaikpe Square.

In the 1970s when the last traditional funeral celebration of our uncle De Job Okoro was held, I was privileged to have been invited by Mazi Kanu Oji – the Eze Aro at Okennachi gathering at Mazi Job Okoro's downstairs parlour. As there was no Onwuchekwa person present, the Eze Aro sent for me and I attended. This was the day that the kindred was informed formally about the forthcoming funeral rite celebration. I must say, that Eze Aro made sure that I was given a prime place in the gathering as an illustrious son of Okennachi and of Nde-Agor compound. Apart from Eze-Aro, Mazi Okereke Izuogu was present at the gathering including the sons of De Job and Chidiebere Okoro – among others.

THE NWAKAMA OKORO'S FACTOR IN OKENNACHI KINDRED MEETING

Before the advent of Dr Nwakama Okoro, Mazi Pius Igboko also of Amuvi Village held sway in Arochukwu affairs. At one time he was the Vice Principal of Aggrey Memorial College Arochukwu and later was a senior lecturer at the University of Nigeria Nsukka. Dr Nwakama Okoro though he returned briefly to Nigeria after his Master of Laws (LL.M) Degree, went back to the United Kingdom for his Doctorate – PHD. I met him at Aba in 1960 at the residence of Mazi Humphrey Okereke Ezuma also of Amuvi Village at Hospital Road, Aba where I resided as a tenant.

When I came to England in 1961, Nwakama was already there; I remembered visiting him in the company of late Barrister Johnson J.A. Okoro at his University. When he eventually returned to Nigeria, it was Mazi Pius Igboko who made him and handed over to him as Secretary of "Nzuko Ikom-na-Inyon Arochukwu". A position, he handled meritoriously. I was not present at the early days of 1970s and would not know whether Nwakama performed any role as regards Okennachi kindred meetings. Perhaps he would have been tutored by Very Rev. Alfred Anicho, and Mazi Pius Igboko both of Amuvi Village and of course Mazi Kanu Oji – the Eze-Aro. When I returned from overseas in late 1973, I met him at Arochukwu in December 1973 – in fact, he came to look for me and took me to the house of Mazi Alex Onyeador where we were entertained. We discussed many things about Arochukwu but Okennachi of the kindred meeting was never discussed.

THE ASCEDANCY OF DR NWAKAMA OKORO

The ascendancy of Dr Nwakama Okoro came when Mazi Kanu Oji, the Eze Aro joined his ancestors in 1987 and there was the urgent necessity for the Okennachi kindred to produce to the Arochukwu Kingdom a new monarch. As I said earlier, Mazi Kanu Oji was the motivator of Okennachi kindred meetings, his passing-on created a great vacuum. Oror Okennachi was alleged to have produced and acknowledged Mazi Vincent Ogbonnaya Okoro Ohu at the Ukwu Ovor (Osim's burial place at Oror) as the Eze-Aro Elect.

Prince Oji Kanu Oji who later became Arianzu-Aro had bowed to his father's dictate in his lifetime never to contest for the Arochukwu throne but to return same to Vincent Ogbonnaya Okoro Ohu whose father passed it on to him. Mazi Oji Kanu Oji also forbade his siblings not to contest for the throne for the same reason.

Thereafter, there appeared to be an incipient murmuring within some elements of Oror Okennachi kindred, who perhaps were prompted by outsiders to contest for the vacant stool. However, Prince Oji Kanu Oji (Arianzu-Aro) stood his grounds and was supported by the majority of Oror Okennachi.

After the Oror Okennachi village presentation of Prince Vincent Okor Ohu as the new Eze-Aro Elect, the Oror members of the kindred presented him to Utugugwu. I was present at that presentation.

Dr Nwakama Okoro SAN, Barrister Johnson Okoro, Mazi Willie Oji of Atani Village, Mazi Obasi Okoronkwo and many other Nde-Agor brothers were in attendance. At this presentation, Prince Vincent Okoro Ohu, in his reply, stated that if even at that stage, he was said not to be entitled to the Arochukwu throne, he would step down. The large crowd shouted in unison that he was entitled. It was then decided that Utugugwu should arrange to present him to Okennachi – home and Diaspora at a date to be arranged. Thereafter,

Okennachi would present him to Ibom Isii kindred and afterwards to Eze-Agwu kindred in that order. It was then arranged by the kindred for the formal presentation of the Prince to the above groups. These events and presentations saw the ascendancy of Dr Nwakama Okoro SAN.

THE EZE ARO SUCCESSION DISPUTE

Nwakama was urged to co-ordinate the activities as an illustrious son of Okennachi. Myself, Mazi Willie Oji, Mazi Obasi Okoronkwo, and Mazi Ezuma Ngwu of Amuvi requested Nwakama to convene a meeting in his house. At this period, one or two sons of Ezeagwu and Ibom Isii started to interfere in the internal affairs and preserve of the Okennachi kindred in the matter of selection and presentation of Eze-Aro Elect to the Aros. Some misguided sons of Okennachi joined the above group and Okennachi kindred rocked. But for the timely intervention of Dr Nwakama Okoro and other well-meaning sons and daughters of the Okennachi kindred who acted as a counterforce, the kindred would have disintegrated or lost cohesion and Arochukwu history would have been in disarray and distorted to the detriment of Okennachi kindred.

A very important Okennachi meeting was convened and consequent upon the resolutions reached there-at, a very powerful protest letter dated 5th April 1988 was addressed to the Secretary-General Ibom Isii Kindred; the Secretary General Eze-Agwu kindred; the President General Nzuko Arochukwu and the General Secretary Nzuko-Arochukwu.

The letter of protest was signed by nine persons as follows:
1. Mazi Oji Kanu Oji – Aria Nzu Aro
2. Mazi Obasi Okoronkwo – Utugugwu
3. Mazi Adimoha Kanu – Asaga
4. Mazi A.O. Aniche – Amuvi
5. Mazi E.E. Chiori – Amangwu
6. Mazi Jacob Nwadibia – Isimkpu
7. Mazi B.O. Kanu – Okennachi Atani

8. Mazi Oke Obasi Onwuchekwa – Okennachi Obinkita

9. Mazi Izuogu Okereke Izuogu – Amankwu and as Secretary General Nzuko Okennachi Kindred.

The above protest letter produced the desired result as Okennachi was asked to produce and introduce Eze-Aro Elect as selected by the kindred for blessing. The Eze-Aro Elect – Mazi Vincent Ogbonnaya Okoro was then presented as follows:

a. Utugugwu presented him to the body of Okennachi kindred on Saturday 5th December 1987 at Eze Aro's Palace Oror;

b. Okennachi presented the Eze-Aro-Elect to the Ibom Isii kindred at Ibom Hall on Saturday (Orie) July 23rd 1988. Eze-Agwu elders were also present at the ceremony. Mazi Goddy Udo of Ibom Village was the Master of Ceremony and Mazi Elder Isaac was Onoh of Agbagwu Village read the welcome address for and on behalf of the Ibom Isii kindred. The Eze-Aro Elect was marshalled from Oror palace to Ibom Hall with "Inyamkpe" and Okonko masquerade followed by a convoy of cars and foot-crowd. Eze-Elect rode in the brand new Mercedes Benz 280SE car belonging to one Atani Okennachi kindred son – Kingsley Okoronkwo Dagogo (Atuu).

Okennachi kindred presented a cow (Evi) and other gifts to the Ibom Isii kindred. I was among the four persons selected to present the cow which was tied outside on a tree. Ibom Isii, in turn, after formal blessing of the new monarch Elect, presented him in a colourful ceremony (mounted by Ibom war dancers), with a large Okwa-Nzu (chalk-trough) for serving kola-nuts to Arochukwu people at his palace.

The Eze Ibom Isii, in his speech, said that in the olden days, the Eze-Elect would have been required to stay for at least four days for his purification, fortification – intellectually and spiritually, diplomatically, physically and supernaturally to be ready to mount the Arochukwu throne. He continued by saying that he is not aware of developments in Arochukwu and as such, he gave the Eze-Elect the blessing of Ibom Isii and admonished him to rule Aro with love, wisdom and uphold the dignity of Arochukwu throne. The Eze-Elect was now escorted back to Oror palace by "Inyamkpe" and "Okonko" now mounted by Ibom Isii Kindred.

c. Presentation to the Eze-Agwu kindred was at a later date at Obinkita Hall. Before the presentation, the question of proper venue, rekindled the old rivalry between Amanagwu and Obinkita. Eventually, it was confirmed that although Agwu-Nwa-Agwu the first son of Mazi Agwu and founder of Amanagwu village, left his fathers' domain at Obinkita to create Amanagwu, yet he insisted before his death that his remains must be taken back to his father's domain for burial – so it was done according to his will.

He was said to have been brought back and buried at Obinkita. So, the three kindreds decided that Obinkita was the proper venue for the presentation of Eze-Aro Elect to the Eze-Agwu kindred; Ibom Isii were also represented at the ceremony.

From the moment of his acceptance and blessing by the last of the three kindreds, Mazi Vincent Ogbonnaya Okoro Ohu became the substantive Eze Aro VIII and no longer Eze-Aro Elect – under a new name of Eze Vincent Ogbonnaya Okoro. I was physically present at the four above presentations at Utughugwu and to the three kindreds.

It is no news that there was a court case challenging Eze-Ogbonnaya Okoro which ended on the 26th July 1995 in favour of Eze Vincent Ogbonnaya Okoro with his closing remark by the presiding judge C.B. U Wogu "May the reign of Eze Aro – Mazi Ogbonnaya Okoro be blessed by our Lord Almighty Amen". The court case is however outside my present narrative and I refer you to a book written by His Royal Majesty:

Eze Ogbonnaya Okoro – "The Journey to the Throne 1988 – 1995".

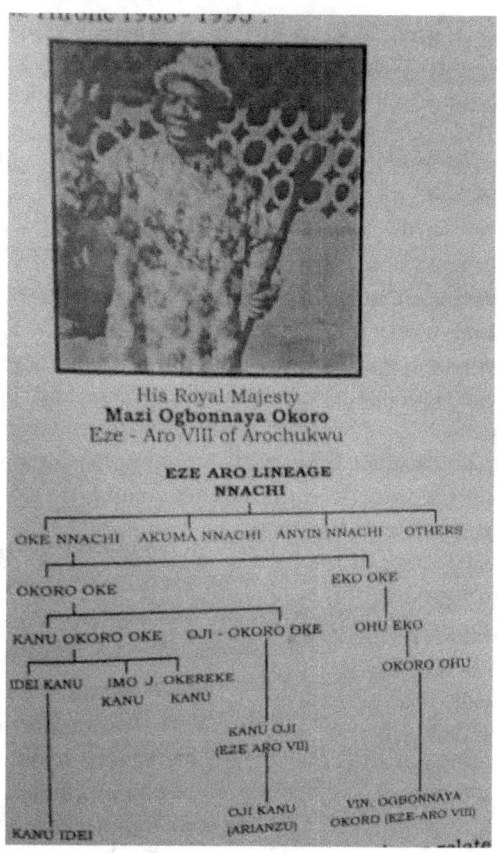

His Royal Majesty
Mazi Ogbonnaya Okoro
Eze - Aro VIII of Arochukwu

The above chart, diagram or graphic perhaps relates to prominent male descendants of Okennachi but does not show the clan of descendants from our original progenitor and descendants of Nnachi. And, even though a woman – HRH Nnene Mgbokwo Udo Omini had ruled Arochukwu over three hundred (300) years ago, this chart is silent on this.

In Paragraph 7 of the Memorandum of Evidence on the status of Chiefs (rulership) in Arochukwu, submitted by the Arochukwu Eze to Professor G. I. Jones; the British Sole Commissioner dated 23rd day of May 1956, and was subsequently incorporated in the Jones' Report on Chieftaincy matters in Eastern Nigeria in 1956 – Nnene Mgbokwo Udo Omini was an Okennachi woman and Monarch.

After the three Arochukwu kindreds had approved and blessed Eze Ogbonnaya Okor, the Nzuko Arochukwu became seized of the matter to uphold what our elders and the kindreds of Arochukwu had anointed, as to do otherwise was to slap the three kindreds of Arochukwu on the face - an abomination. So, whether the three kindreds' decision was right or wrong, it had the blessing of the ancestors. Nzuko Arochukwu then defended the case filed against the Eze Elect – in other words Arochukwu Kingdom. Dr Nwakama Okoro SAN volunteered his services free of charge and his junior was our own son (Nde Agor son) Barrister Johnson Okoro.

I told Nwakama Okoro that I could not be coming from Lagos for the case with its attendant and frequent court adjournments. That I had made my own humble contribution by attending most of the kindred meetings convened, all the way from Lagos.

Throughout the brouhaha, Dr Nwakama Okoro gave of his means, his time and his all. I attended several Okennachi kindred meetings convened in his residence at the time. Nwakama did not at any time talk-down or intimidate any of those present. He did not show off his wealth, he did not seek relevance but relevance was thrust on him by circumstance of the death of Mazi Kanu Oji, Eze-Aro VII in 1987. Nwakama was a Senior Advocate of Nigeria (SAN), he was a politician and had contested for the Governorship of Imo State under NPN although he lost to late Sam Mbakwe of the NPP. At the time NPN was not popular in Imo State due to the Dr Nnamdi Azikiwe factor. He was at home, the Secretary General of Nzuko Aro under Mazi Paul Okoro as President General. He was widely known in Nigeria.

However, as a human being, Nwakama might have made some mistakes (unknown to me) in his handling of Arochukwu matters – "to err is human". Only those who come forward to serve that make mistakes those who sit on the fence and criticise have no way of proving their leadership and organisational prowess. Nwakama was a good Aro son. However, he passed-away before the final determination of the court case for which he had laboured. May his soul rest in perfect peace. Amen.

CONCLUSION

I must use this opportunity to thank the following Nde-Agor brothers of Lagos Branch for urging me to put pen to paper in this work: Architect Chima Chijoke, Pharamacist Udo Chijoke, Geologist P.C. Okoro (at the time of writing he was President of Lagos Branch), Pastor Alex Onwuchekwa and Assistant Superintendant of Police Gabriel Onwuchekwa.

Any misstatement of historical facts and other errors in this material is due entirely to me of which I accept full responsibility. I am aware of the saying that "little knowledge is dangerous" but I am also aware of the wider saying that "half bread is better than none". Okennachi kindred meeting did not start with Dr Nwakama Okoro although his role in this regard was invaluable.

OKENNACHI IN OBINKITA:

Politically, administratively, demographically, and geographically, Nde-Agor compound is part of Obinkita Village and has been since living memory, playing a yeoman's role in financial and all activities of Obinkita Village. But, for the purpose of kindred formation in participating in the selection of Arochukwu Monarch, Nde-Agor is Okennachi and indeed a prominent arm of the kindred as we are homologous to Oror palace which we should endeavour to support at all times, by good advice and counselling and by ensuring that we do not unwittingly join in the chorus of detractors of the Arochukwu throne and thereby undermining our heritage.

AROCHUKWU BURIAL CUSTOM

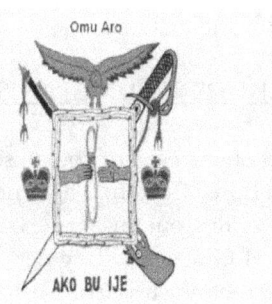

By Barrister George M. Onwuchekwa Esq.

("Ugwu-Aro")

Written: 10th October 2003

EXTRACTS FROM A LETTER BY THE AUTHOR TO HIS WIFE AND CHILDREN

10th October 2003.

My dear wife and children,

Re: AROCHUKWU BURIAL CUSTOM

I enclose a copy to each of you on some important aspects of Arochukwu Burial Custom. I have no premonition of death whatsoever in writing out this guide, but I am merely doing so at the request of Grace (my daughter) who wants me to give a guide as to Arochukwu Burial Custom Rites. And, I thank her so much for doing this because most of you [the family members] who grew up outside the Ancient Town of Arochukwu should be properly guided in the event of the inevitable – so as not to play into the hands of jobbers, customary law nincompoops and other armchair advisers……

As I said, this is merely a guide and your further questions would enable me to clarify some grey areas.

Yours affectionately,

George .M. Onwuchekwa Esq

FOREWORD

My father was a fountain of knowledge on all aspects of Arochukwu custom thanks to having grown up in Aroversity (Arochukwu University of Understanding) under the tutelage of his erudite and knowledgeable father (my grandfather) Teacher Moses Onwuchekwa. The article or essay you are about to read was written by him more than fifteen [15] years before his transition to glory at the request of my sister Mrs Grace Julia Okoroji. Extracts from the cover letter accompanying it clarify the context for its production.

Since this document was produced, Arochukwu custom has inevitably evolved slightly with regard to the cost and brand of some items required to fulfil the customary demands. In this regard I am grateful to various family members who assisted with plugging the gaps. For instance where Schnapps (Gin) is mentioned in my father's write-up this has been replaced with either whiskey or brandy. The monetary amounts accompanying the cultural items have also increased due to currency fluctuation. Where there have been changes I have exercised my liberty as editor to insert the revised amounts or items as well as commentary in square brackets. All references to the "author's son" refer to me and are made by me in the third person.

Apart from these variations, the content of my father's write-up despite its age remains valid and authoritative within the context of Okennachi Kindred and I can testify to this having just fulfilled the burial rites obligations for him. I found it useful having advance knowledge of the process even though I deferred to my extended family in certain areas. I understand that different kindred, families and villages may have variations which have been cultivated over time. This paper does not discredit such variations or seek to dispute their authenticity. If anything it seeks to complement them as a venerable part of Arochukwu customary rites for burials. As the author clarifies in his letter to us, it is merely a guide, but it is one that we (his widow and children) are willing to share for the benefit of the community particularly those Aro citizens in Diaspora.

I therefore commend this write-up to you and pray that it provides a reliable navigational guide around the various pit falls awaiting the uninitiated when laying their loved ones to rest in our beloved Ancient Town of Arochukwu.

God Bless you.

Barrister Joseph Amaeze Esq (the author's son)

2nd November 2019

AROCHUKWU BURIAL CUSTOM

The Aros bury their deceased loved ones in the family premises and depending on the status of the deceased, and relationship, the deceased is buried in the family home. If the deceased had his own house at Arochukwu, he and his wife are buried in the house whenever each respective death occurs. The husband, who is the head of his family, is buried in his room and likewise the wife is buried in her room or other prominent room. In some families, or at the request of the deceased themselves during their lifetimes, the deceased may be buried in his or her forecourt. Today, because of the ugly incidence of miscreants tampering with the corpse, it is advisable not to do so; as a result many do bury their parents inside the house.

STEPS:

1. [a] **ANNOUNCEMENT**

Where the death occurs at Arochukwu, the announcement of death is made by the immediate family. Usually it is the eldest male in the family or extended family who will be directed to make the official announcement. Where the deceased has a grown-up son, and he is available at home, he takes charge in consultation with the elders of the family. If he is not readily available and in particular if the sons are overseas, urgent messages must be sent to him or them by relations or close family friends and the burial does not take place until he or they arrive. The body must however, be embalmed in a reputable hospital's morgue [mortuary] for preservation. There are such morgues at Umuahia and at Aba.

[b] Announcement after the burial date had been determined in consultation with elders and relations are made as follows:-

[i] **FAMILY COMPOUND**: Convene the family gathering at Arochukwu and the Compound gathering and inform them officially of the burial date and other arrangements for the conveyance of the corpse back to Arochukwu and for burial. The family meeting is given "Ngwa-Ato" which consists of an arm of goat or bush meat [not grass-cutter], one small jar of palm wine, one bottle of Schnapps [Now a bottle of whiskey/brandy], kola nuts [4 Igbo kola] and Okwu-ose and a crate of soft drinks/minerals [Now a crate of malt].

For the Compound Meeting, you present "Ngwa-Isii", consisting of an arm and a leg of dried meat or goat, a full jar of palm wine, 2 bottles of Schnapps [Now whiskey or brandy – the family will advise on the brand but it is usually St Remi or similar], and two crates of soft drinks/minerals [Now 2 crates of Malt drink]. People who have do more according to their financial capability. Then help is solicited from the Compound members for physical assistance throughout the burial.

[ii] **VILLAGE MEN AND WOMEN**: A bottle of Schnapps [Now whisky or brandy] is taken to inform the Eze-Ogo of the particular village [this has changed and depends on village and family – the author's son provided a bottle of brandy plus a sum of money to inform the Eze of his village.] Once this has been received by the Eze-Ogo he is given some details of the burial arrangement. In some villages he is requested to send the village grave diggers and for this another bottle of Schnapps [Now brandy or whisky] is given to him for the invitation.

By custom, it is the Village that is responsible for grave-digging. There is a group of young men to do this. The group are entertained with drinks etc. However, today many people employ their own grave-diggers, but this has led to quarrels between such families and their village; [the author's son was instructed by elders to use young men from the family compound to dig the grave and for this purpose he provided a bottle of whiskey, plus a sum of money].

[In some villages the first son or child is given the pick axe to break the floor area where the grave is going to be dug before the grave diggers commence work. This is symbolical.]

After the grave has been dug, the family may decide to cement its walls. After blocking [using a mason to create an inner wall with cement blocks within the grave to fortify the foundation of the house], the family may decide to decorate the grave in accordance with what they wish for their dearly departed parents or loved ones. The village womenfolk are also informed through their leader with a bottle of Schnapps [Now whisky or brandy to which may add a crate of Malt as some women no longer drink alcohol]. The women have a role to play, particularly in properly solidifying the grave [Ikuchi-Ili] about 2 days after burial and for this they are properly fed and entertained.

[iii] **EZE-ARO**: Eze Aro of Arochukwu must be formally informed when the sons arrive. They should pay him homage with a bottle of Schnapps [Now whisky or brandy plus a carton of beer, a crate of malt and a sum of money] and other drink items and then he is officially briefed about all the arrangements. He may want to know whether the family, the Compound [Utugiyi] and the village have been properly informed in that order. Eze Aro's palace and other kindred may also be informed.

[iv] **NOTIFYING KINDRED**: - Burial is the biggest industry in Arochukwu, like many other rural communities, and costs money as some people want to be entertained without contributing anything. The deceased's Kindred [Okennachi, Eze-agwu and Ibom Isii] may also need to be informed. Such information should include a bottle of hot drink (whisky or brandy plus a sum of money).

[v] **IN-LAWS**:- the deceased's in-laws from (a) his maternal/mother's side of the family (b) his wife's family and (c) where he has sons and daughters-in-law, all these need to be informed and this is usually done with a bottle of Schnapps (Now whisky or brandy] to the heads of the respective families.

[vi] **SOCIETIES AND ASSOCIATIONS**:- where the deceased was involved with various local societies and organisations within Arochukwu, such as youth groups, social clubs, and community partnerships, all these need to be informed with a bottle of hot drink [whisky or brandy along with a crate of Malt/soft drink if so desired] for each group delivered through the head of that group or association. NZUKO ARO will also need to be informed with a bottle of hot drink (whisky or brandy plus a sum of money.)

[vii] **EKPE SOCIETY**:- if the deceased was a member of "Ekpe Na Mboko", the Ekpe Society may want to send a delegation to the family to ask about their position in the whole affair. They may even threaten to disrupt the burial. They should be appeased with bottles of hot drinks [whisky or brandy] and a sum of money and be informed that after the Church or Christian burial, the family will consult them at a convenient time to either plan a Traditional Ekpe Burial or discuss their demands. Of course, this may never actually take place particularly where the deceased is a devout Christian who has either renounced or distanced themselves from Ekpe Society activity.

2. **MODALITIES FOR BURIAL**:

- [i] **CASKET [COFFIN]**: To be bought by the first son or by the children and not by an outsider or other member of the family . It is the children's duty to bury their father or mother.
- [ii] **COW**: Depending on the status of the deceased, a cow is a must – a cow must be slaughtered in accordance with Arochukwu custom and failure to do this is frowned upon. In many instances more than one cow can be slaughtered depending on the means of the deceased's family. Some who cannot afford a healthy sizeable cow have opted for either a smaller cow (symbolical) or half of a cow accompanied by the slaughtering of other livestock such as goats and rams.

After all it is often said in some quarters that a poor man's goat is his cow. However, none of these is deemed an appropriate substitute. Some onlookers have been known to mock smaller cows and refer to them as the senior brother of a goat which is a disparaging remark to make. But, it is acknowledged that a burial is the last chance of the living to honour the dead and that it is an occasion for one to put their best foot forward regardless of the expense. The cow must be a healthy size [many opt for a young male cow because the flesh is said to be very tender]. Traditionally the cow must be covered with an unbroken length of Indian madras [George material] wrapped around its torso and cannot be slaughtered until the deceased's body arrives at his final resting place. This is symbolical.

3. **PREPARING THE CORPSE FOR BURIAL**:-

[i] If the death occurred at Arochukwu and everyone is at home, the burial could take place within a few days of death where embalmment is either at the deceased's home or in an Arochukwu mortuary. It is usually the daughter with the assistance of her mother who will wash and dress the corpse before it lies in state; [there are variations to this theme where a deceased can stipulate during their lifetime others whom they wish to be involved in this process such as a favoured daughter-in-law or favourite sister].

[ii] If death occurred outside Arochukwu (elsewhere within Nigeria or overseas), after embalmment, in the morning when the corpse will be conveyed to Arochukwu, the hospital authorities may prepare the deceased's corpse for an additional sum of money. To facilitate the preparation of the corpse the mortuary or hospital authorities will be given the casket and clothing to be worn. It is usual however for some close relatives to be present whilst this is being done.

4. **MOVEMENT OF THE DECEASED'S BODY (STOP-OVERS):-**

[i] **Ambulance**: This is to be hired by the family for conveying the body to Arochukwu (where death occurred outside the town) and then either the same ambulance or another one for conveying the body along the route for the various flagstops that are required by custom before arriving at the final resting place or place where the body will be lying in state. The ambulance is also required to convey the corpse between the place of lying in state and the church and then back to the final resting place on the day of funeral. [These days the preference is for an ambulance with loud siren which has different modes for special sound effects]. Such ambulance can be hired in Arochukwu at daily rate.

[ii] **Stop-over/Flag Stops**: Whether the deceased died in Aro or elsewhere it is customary for the body in the casket to be conveyed around Arochukwu prior to lying-in-state. [the author's son learnt that in some villages and/or kindred, depending on the deceased person's status, where such person died outside the town the earliest their corpse can arrive in Arochukwu is late afternoon. This is to enable people gather to receive the corpse in a befitting way. As most of people are out in their farm or trading during the day, the stop overs had to wait until evening].

The ambulance conveying the deceased accompanied by vehicles belonging to family and well-wishers forms the head of a convoy as it makes its way to significant locations, which were relevant during the life of the deceased. The usual starting point for this journey is Nkwu-Nabu "T" junction. Once the convoy is assembled at this point the journey to the final resting place commences. Some may also choose to carry a dance troupe of young men and women and their musicians. Some families employ the firing of cannons (operated by igniting gunpowder) at each flag stop or stop over to announce the arrival of the deceased.

The flag stops or stop-over places are usually to the deceased's in-laws (if either he or any of his children married into an Aro family), the deceased's maternal lineage (mother's village and family compound if she was from Aro), Eze Aro's palace at Oror Village and then their ancestral (father's) home where the casket is opened for the family to observe. The casket is not opened in any other of the flag stops or stop-overs. It is only opened at the ancestral home. The stop over at the ancestral home is because this is where the deceased was either born or grew up and is a mark of respect to his father, the extended family and the family compound.

At each of the flag stops a bottle of hot drink plus 4 Igbo kola-nuts are given to the elders who receive the deceased and gather around the ambulance whilst prayers and salutations are made in memory of the deceased. At the ancestral home however there is breaking of kola and pouring of libation in addition to the prayer. The family then escort the deceased to his final resting place to lie-in-state. On arrival at the place for lying-in-state, the body will be received by the family and again one bottle of hot drink (whisky or brandy) plus 4 Igbo kola-nuts are provided.

5. **LYING IN STATE AND WAKE-KEEPING**:

Lying in State: this usually takes place in the parlour of the deceased's home which should be decorated with George cloth including Omu-Aro and white lace materials. A platform should be erected and decorated with white lace or a large raised bed also decorated with lace for the deceased to lie-in state. The deceased will either remain in the casket which may be partially open [these days there are caskets with a clear Perspex screen so that the upper torso of the deceased can be seen whilst remaining protected beneath the screen. Photos of the deceased should adorn the walls. There should also be a condolence register with the deceased's portrait displayed prominently along with a biro [ball point pen].

Wake-keeping should normally be at the deceased's residence. For Christians there should be a Gospel Band, and in addition to any other form of entertainment including traditional dances, musicians, and other forms of entertainment. It is usual for a Christian service to be conducted with a choir in attendance where the deceased was a Christian and thereafter for more traditional forms of wake-keeping to take place, including serving of refreshments. The deceased's daughter will usually dance carrying her father's enlarged framed portrait accompanied by other women from the family and community including in-laws.

In the olden days, it was usual for the widow to sit on the bare floor overnight besides the deceased's casket but these days a foam mattress is used properly covered and decorated along with a pillow where she may sit and sleep with close relations always by her side. Although in times past widows had to shave their heads as a mark of mourning but this practise has been stopped by many enlightened Aro people who decide the best way to mourn the deceased.

At the wake-keeping there is eating and drinking into the early hours and music is always present. Whilst it is not usual to cook food during the wake-keeping but to serve snacks such as meat pie or puff-puff, however because many guests travel in from far and have not had time to eat it is sensible to budget for preparing food for them.

6. **FUNERAL SERVICE**:

For Christians, the funeral commences with a church service in the morning. Due to people arriving from different places this may usually start late morning to give them time to assemble in the church pews. Before announcing the burial date it is important that there should be concrete arrangement made with the church priest, reverend, bishop or pastor. Failure to iron out the details of the church service early enough could result in frustration of the funeral plans. Some families choose instead to invite a pastor or priest to officiate the funeral service in their family compounds or residential premises where they are unable to obtain a slot in the church calendar. For instance the funeral of Dr Nwakanma Okoro SAN was conducted at his premises, so there are precedents for this form of religious ceremony. These days if you can afford it you should hire and pay for the services of some armed police in case trouble makers want to disrupt the ceremony.

7. **IKPUYI-AKU [COVERING OF CLOTH]**:

On the burial morning, a table should be set aside by the Compound or family and another one for the village. Visitors and relations who intend to cover the deceased with cloth or other condolence gifts will go and make their presentation.

[a] Family Members:- Wife, son with daughter-in-law and daughter with son-in-law must each present a fathom of George cloth. They do not donate cash or hot drinks as that is for other relations and friends. The George cloth given by the wife, the son and his wife, daughter and her husband are used to cover the top of the corpse before the casket is finally covered of sealed. These go down with the deceased as last honour. All other cloths are preserved and become property of the wife, the daughter and the daughter-in-law as may eventually be distributed by the wife.

[b] Other Donations:- Full names of donors, the nature and amount of donation is properly recorded. This is Mgbaru and it is important for the purpose of expressing gratitude afterwards to all those who generously gave. In your compound, some of the condolence cash gifts go to the compound and extended family and 50% of all donations except the ones people made at the village table is for the immediate family and to be handed over to the first son as he may deem fit.

All gifts from in-laws are exclusively to the immediate family and should be handed over to the first son or if there are no sons then the first daughter who will accept them and thank the in-laws.

[c] Entertainment for guests particularly in-laws, dignitaries such as Eze-Aro and members of the ruling council should be a priority. Usually they are catered for in separate canopies from the generality of attendees.

8. CATERING [FOR THE CEREMONY]:

At Arochukwu today many people hire professional party cooks. Most villages have these service providers who render such service on payment. By shopping around and avoiding sentiment for cooks from one's own compound or village you should be able to secure a good caterer for a reasonable price. They always have their own pots, tripods and other utensils, but a vehicle must be arranged for conveying them to and fro the venue. By using professionals you will avoid argument and quarrel by the womenfolk within your own compound.

CONCLUSION

It is difficult to state everything on paper and one cannot provide for every eventuality. But, be prudent, be patient and listen to good counselling of trusted elders within your family and do your best. Do not impoverish yourself however because you must carry on living after the funeral and care for your own family. Expenditure on burial is a dead investment as it does not yield any dividend or earthly returns. The important thing is to honour your parents as commanded by the Bible.

The object of writing out the above is merely to give you an insight into Arochukwu custom on the subject of burial. Unfortunately there are many so-called elders who do not know or even understand Arochukwu custom. When they see a wealthy family, they interpret Arochukwu Village or Compound custom to suit their greed and expectation. There may be several interpretations as each elder calls a member of the family aside to brain-wash and dupe him or her into accepting his interpretation and for him to be the go-between.

It is unfortunately a sign of the times that burial has become one of the biggest industries in rural communities where some families unwittingly play into the hands of some of these so-called elders whose stock-in-trade is to feed fat on other people's misery whilst pretending to be assisting. It was not always so. It is therefore for you to know what you want to do and implement it even if you are called all sorts of names – that should not bother any sensible person who understands Aro. You should calmly and politely tell the arm-chair adviser that you have heard and thank him before going away to implement your already mapped-out plan. Under no circumstances should you insult the elder even where he becomes unbearable and a pest or pain-in-the-neck or is causing disruption. Everyone will forget what the elder said or did to provoke your reaction and will instead focus their attention on your insult which may then result in family quarrel that creates a distraction. As the Bible says, God resists the proud but gives grace to the humble. So be humble submit to God and He will direct your paths.

God Bless you.

Your Father,

George .M. Onwuchekwa Esq

"Ugwu Aro" and "Iyi-Ukwu Obinkita"

THE ODYSSEY
OF
GEORGE MOSES ONWUCHEKWA

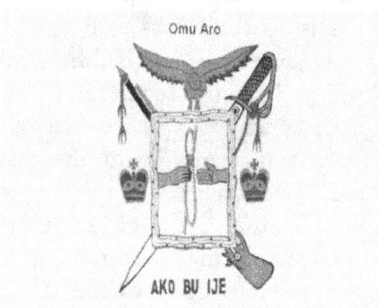

By George M. Onwuchekwa Esq.

(Ugwu-Aro)

Written: 2002

ODYSSEY OF GEORGE MOSES ONWUCHEKWA

GEORGE MOSES ONWUCHEKWA was born at Ndi-Agor Compound of Obinkita Village, Arochukwu Town on the 18th of December 1934. He was the second son and third child of his parents, the late Elder Teacher Moses Onwuchekwa and his wife late Madam Grace Mgbokwo Onwuchekwa. His father was one of the earliest Teacher/black missionaries having had his own education at the Hope Waddell Training Institute, Calabar where he graduated Higher Elementary Teacher (Grade II Teacher) in 1925. Later, he was conferred with the Senior Teachers Certificate by the Government of the Federation of Nigeria. George's mother – the late Madam Grace Mgbokwo Onwuchekwa was one of the earliest pupils of the Slessor Memorial Home established by the Scottish Women Missionaries from where she graduated a Domestic Science Teacher of yester-years. The marriage of George's parents, on the 17th day of March 1927 was the first ever Church Marriage in Arochukwu and the beginning of Church Marriages in Arochukwu Town.

Being a son of a teacher cum missionary, George went to school early and followed his father wherever he was transferred to by the Mission except for a short interregnum when he was forced as part of his training (which was common in those days) to go and live with immediate relations of his parents.

EARLY LIFE AND EDUCATION:

Young George started his education at the Church of Scotland Mission School, Obinkita, Arochukwu [now Arochukwu Central School] at the age of four [4] years old in January 1939, but was uprooted the same year when he was forced to go and live with his paternal cousin. He attended the All Saints School, Umukurushe near Port Harcourt, 1940 – 1942; then

Asaga Ohafia Mission School [Headed by his father] from 1942 - 1945. It was in this school that he met Dr Uma Eleazu and the Mmaduekwes who are his long time bosom friends. He then went to Ohafia Central School from January 1946 to June 1946 and then to Amaodu Ututu Mission School near Arochukwu Town when he was forced once again to go and live with a maternal uncle. In 1948 he returned to Abiriba Mission School headed by his father and transferred with his father in 1949 back to Arochukwu Mission School from where his educational pilgrimage began.

Barrister George Moses Onwuchekwa attended the Zik's Institute Ontisha for his Secondary Education between 1950 and 1953 [for his G.C.E O'Level]. There was along break as was the pattern in those days when he had to go and work for a living before preparing to sail to the United Kingdom to read Law as there was no faculty of Law then in the only Nigerian University – University College Ibadan. He eventually sailed to the United Kingdom in 1961 in spite of the fact that he had just been promoted Executive Officer by the Royal Exchange Assurance – the dominant Insurance British Corporation in Nigeria at that time.

He enrolled at the North Western Polytechnic in September 1961 for his G.C.E. A 'Level and passed in Economics, Economic History and British Constitution with good grades. It was at this Institution that he met some of his friends namely Hon. Justice Ikechi Ogbuagu; Barrister John Obonna; Mr and Mrs Aboderin, the founder of Punch Newspapers; and many others.

He attended full-time Holborn College of Law between 1962 and 1965 and graduated with an LL.B of the University of London with Second Class Upper Honours. He then attended the University College – University of London 1965 to 1966 and graduated LL.M [Master of Laws] with Distinction in Company Law. George attended a short course at The Hague Academy of International Law, Peace Palace [International Court of Justice] Hague, Holland in 1965 and was awarded the Short Course Certificate. Called to the

English Bar as a Barrister at Michaelmas Term 1968 by the Honourable Gray's Inn.

After teaching and practising in England as a Barrister/Lecturer, George returned to Nigeria in September 1973 to assume Lectureship position at the Faculty of Law, University of Lagos and at the same time attending the Nigerian Law School between 1973 and 1974 under special dispensation; because of his previous teaching and practice experience in England he was allowed to combine the two programmes at the same time. George was made a Notary Public by the Supreme Court of Nigeria on the 30th day of June 1980. He then became a full-member of the Nigerian Institute of Management (MNIM) in 1995; and a Member of the Nigerian Council of International Chamber of Commerce on 16th February 1988.

WORK PROFILE:

George started his working life as a Tutor something he relished and which encompassed a sizeable proportion of his working life. Even when he stopped formal teaching he remained a tutor at heart seizing every opportunity to dispense learning and support development within any community he found himself. His work profile is as follows:

1. Tutor Eastern Missionary College, Ikot Ekpene now in Akwa Ibom State, from 1956 to 1957;

2. Assistant Principal Clerk /Executive Officer at Royal Exchange Assurance Lagos from 1957 to 1961;

3. Boys Placement Officer, Inner London Education - Youths Employment Service and Career Office London 1966 to 1967;

4. Lecturer in Company and Commercial Law between 1968 and May 1970 [specialising in Company Law; Executorship, Estate Duty and Bankruptcy] at North East London Polytechnic [Now University of North East London];

5. Permanent Tutor and Lecturer, June 1970 to September 1973 at Council of Legal Education, the Inns of Court School of Law, Grays Inn London [The first African to

be employed on full-time basis at that distinguished and ancient British Institution of Law];

6. Senior Lecturer in Commercial Law at the Faculty of Law, University of Lagos between September 1973 and September 1978;

7. Examiner in Law for the Nigerian Institute of Bankers between 1978 and 1981.

LEGAL PRACTICE:

George Moses Onwuchekwa served first six months Pupillage after his call to the English Bar under Mr Neil Taylor Q.C (at No.2 Dr Johnsons Building) Temple, London in 1970 and the second six months pupillage under Victor Durrand Q.C. in Queen Elizabeth Building, Temple, London in 1971.

George was later called to the Nigerian Bar in July 1974 and was made a Notary Public for Nigeria by the Supreme Court in 1980.

George was a part-time consultant on Corporate and Commercial law to Chief Rotimi Williams Chambers between 1975 and 1978, and went on to occupy a full-time position as consultant to the same chambers between 1978 and 1981 when he amicably severed his official relationship with Chief Rotimi Williams Chambers. George continued to be a good friend with the Chambers and a senior member of the Chief Williams Black Table.

George was at one time also a part-time consultant to Chief Godfrey Amachree Q.C. George started his own Law firm from 1981 to 2004 and travelled globally in connection with his legal practice.

An avid writer, George also wrote many learned articles on Law in Nigerian and international journals, delivered Law papers at various workshops and conferences, and was the first Editor-in-Chief of the Butterworth Publication's Law Reports of Nigeria.

PUBLIC SERVICE:

Barrister George Moses Onwuchekwa was appointed a Director of the Federal Government owned Nigerian Bank for Commerce and Industry by the Murtala Muhammed/Obasanjo military regime from 1976 to 1979; he was subsequently appointed Chairman Board of directors of National Electric Power Authority [NEPA] between 1985 and 1986 under the Buhari/Idiagbon military regime.

In 1992 (4th November 1992) he was a Ministerial Honour Award winner in recognition of his Contribution and Support towards the development and growth of the Electricity Industry in Nigeria.

In terms of roles, George Moses Onwuchekwa was:

1. Director of United Geophysical Nigeria Limited between 1978 and 1988;

2. Director of DPMS Limited (formerly IBM Nigeria Ltd) between 1986 and 2005;

3. President Lagos [Doyen] Lions Club for the 2001/2002 Lionistic Year;

4. Prior to being president he was Chairman Membership Committee and Chairman Constitution Committee of the Club;

5. A member of Arochukwu Social Club of Nigeria [ARSCON] between 1985 and 2019;

6. Patron Nzuko Arochukwu, Lagos Branch;

7. Patron Obinkita Progressive Union;

8. Patron Ezi Enyi Social Club of Nigeria;

9. Patron Federated Arochukwu Youth Association 1984 to 2019;

10. Councillor in Eze-Aro Advisory Council – the body of advisors to the Arochukwu Monarch;

11. Member Nigeria Economic Summit Group

"UGWU-ARO"

On the 26th of December 2000, because of George Moses Onwuchekwa's years of service and contribution to the development of Arochukwu Town, the Arochukwu Monarch His Majesty Eze Ogbonnaya Okoro CPR, Eze Aro VIII and the Arochukwu Town Union [Nzuko Arochukwu] conferred on him the prestigious title of "UGWU-ARO" which is the highest honour Arochukwu Kingdom confers on some of its citizens.

PERSONAL LIFE

Barrister George Moses Onwuchekwa married his heart-throb Miss Mary Magdalen Udoma, a then Health-Visitor and subsequently an Inspector of Nursing Schools, on the 10 July 1965 at St Joseph's catholic Monastery, Highgate Hill, London. The marriage is blessed with a son Barrister Joseph Amaeze and a daughter Mrs Grace Julia Chinyere Okoroji (a Research Scientist and Christian Counsellor) who are both happily married. George and Mary are blessed with 6 grandchildren who are all successful in their various endeavours.

George's intimacy with his wife extended to them sharing pet names. His fond pet name for her was "my Poggy Bonnie" and hers for him was "Adam". The secret behind those nicknames remains a closely guarded secret. Apart from bringing up and caring for his nuclear family, George was very generous to his brothers, sisters and other members of his extended family and his in-laws also. George contributed to the welfare and burial of his parents and parents-in-law and immortalized his father's name through various donations to schools and charities. He was a devout Christian who placed his faith in God and tried to live according to scriptural instruction. He was also committed to the work of the faith and contributed to the construction and development of several churches he attended.

MATTERS ARISING

It would appear that I have painted in glowing terms what I consider to be my achievements. These achievements, (if they may be called so), were not accomplished by sudden flight, but were the concomitant of persistent hard work, perseverance, endurance and sometimes of lost hope and helplessness. My chequered history has made me sober, humble and reflective. My wide travel has enabled me to see the world at its best (in the developed countries of Europe and in the United States) and at its worst (in some parts of Africa), that I have learnt the lesson of contentment and become more prayerful and more thankful to Almighty God. I am equally more compassionate to the less privileged and downtrodden.

Perhaps, these were my motivations in joining the Lions Club. To join hands with other well-meaning people to do what cannot be done alone. During my presidency of the Lagos chapter of the Club 2001/2002 various humanitarian activities were undertaken including donations of large quantities of vitally needed drugs and antibiotics to community clinics, donations of toiletries to impoverished communities and visits to the old-peoples' homes.

My life has been a joy to me no matter where I go, I have learnt to live in harmony with every friend and foe. In my life, I have had privilege and honour to meet and associate with some good people who have touched my life in one way or another, both at home and abroad. I thank you all jointly and severally for touching my life.

George .M. Onwuchekwa Esq

Arochukwu: A Patriarch's Reflections

Arochukwu: A Patriarch's Reflections is a compilation of books and essays penned by the hand of the late George Moses Onwuchekwa a Barrister at Law, budding historian and expert in the customs and traditions of the great nation of Arochukwu. Born and brought up in Arochukwu in the early 20th century, and blessed with photographic memory, G. M. Onwuchekwa spent time in what he calls Aroversity (the Arochukwu University of Understanding) under his father's tutelage. The books cover the genesis of Aro, its marriage customs, the history of the ruling lineage and his childhood memories of the place, its people and their customs. Whilst this is not strictly an academic historical, geographical or anthropological piece it nevertheless provides a reliable stepping stone to those venturing into the study of Arochukwu from those disciplines. For those with no academic aspirations in relation to Aro but who wish to know more about it, it is a rich source of useful information and insight. As the author clarifies, he has written from what he saw with his eyes (his experience) and heard with his ears (by way of oral tradition). The books included here are Arochukwu Marriage Customs, Arochukwu Land of my Birth, Arochukwu Golden Years, and The Okennachi Kindred. It also contains an essay on Arochukwu burial custom and his brief autobiography which provides a snapshot of the accomplishments of a literary genius and incisive historian.